COMBINING CASE STUDY DESIGNS FOR THEORY BUILDING

Case study research is a versatile approach that allows for different data sources to be combined, with its main purpose being theory development. This book goes a step further by combining different case study research designs, informed by the authors' extensive teaching and research experience. It provides an accessible introduction to case study research, familiarizes readers with different archetypical and sequenced designs, and describes these designs and their components using both real and fictional examples. It provides thought-provoking exercises and, in doing so, prepares the reader to design their own case study in a way that suits the research objective. Written for an academic audience, this book is useful for students, their supervisors and professors, and ultimately any researcher who intends to use, or is already using, the case study approach.

LAKSHMI BALACHANDRAN NAIR is Assistant Professor in the Department of Business and Management at LUISS Guido Carli University, Italy. Her research interests include qualitative methodology, business ethics, and organization studies. She has published journal articles, case studies, book chapters, and books on these topics. She has received several awards and grants, including the BAM Best Paper Award (2022) and the ECRM Teaching Research Methods Excellence Award (2022).

MICHAEL GIBBERT is Professor of Sustainable Consumption at the University of Lugano, Switzerland. He has more than 20 years of experience in teaching qualitative methods and has received numerous prizes at renowned conferences.

BAREERAH HAFEEZ HOORANI is Assistant Professor of Qualitative Empirical Methods at Nijmegen School of Management, Radboud University, the Netherlands. Her research focuses on qualitative research methods and organizational identity. She has been the recipient of numerous best paper awards at the British Academy of Management conferences.

T0370773

COMBINING CASE STUDY DESIGNS FOR THEORY BUILDING

A New Sourcebook for Rigorous Social Science Researchers

LAKSHMI BALACHANDRAN NAIR

LUISS Guido Carli University

MICHAEL GIBBERT

Università della Svizzera Italiana

BAREERAH HAFEEZ HOORANI

Radboud University

CAMBRIDGE
UNIVERSITY PRESS

Shaftesbury Road, Cambridge CB2 8EA, United Kingdom

One Liberty Plaza, 20th Floor, New York, NY 10006, USA

477 Williamstown Road, Port Melbourne, VIC 3207, Australia

314–321, 3rd Floor, Plot 3, Splendor Forum, Jasola District Centre, New Delhi – 110025, India

103 Penang Road, #05–06/07, Visioncrest Commercial, Singapore 238467

Cambridge University Press is part of Cambridge University Press & Assessment, a department of the University of Cambridge.

We share the University's mission to contribute to society through the pursuit of education, learning and research at the highest international levels of excellence.

www.cambridge.org
Information on this title: www.cambridge.org/9781316519295

DOI: 10.1017/9781009023283

First published 2023

A catalogue record for this publication is available from the British Library.

Library of Congress Cataloging-in-Publication Data
NAMES: Nair, Lakshmi Balachandran, author. | Gibbert, Michael, author. | Hoorani, Bareerah Hafeez, author.
TITLE: Combining case study designs for theory building : a new sourcebook for rigorous social science researchers / Lakshmi Balachandran Nair, LUISS Guido Carli University of Rome, Michael Gibbert, Università della Svizzera Italiana, Bareerah Hafeez Hoorani, Radboud University.
DESCRIPTION: 1 Edition. | New York, NY : Cambridge University Press, 2023. | Includes bibliographical references and index.
IDENTIFIERS: LCCN 2022033963 (print) | LCCN 2022033964 (ebook) | ISBN 9781316519295 (hardback) | ISBN 9781009010245 (paperback) | ISBN 9781009023283 (epub)
SUBJECTS: LCSH: Social sciences–Research–Case studies. | Social sciences–Methodology.
CLASSIFICATION: LCC H62 .N243 2023 (print) | LCC H62 (ebook) | DDC 300.72–dc23/eng/20220914
LC record available at https://lccn.loc.gov/2022033963
LC ebook record available at https://lccn.loc.gov/2022033964

ISBN 978-1-316-51929-5 Hardback
ISBN 978-1-009-01024-5 Paperback

Contents

CHAPTER I

Introduction to Case Study Research

1.1   History

In the eighteenth century, French sociologist Pierre Guillaume Frederic Le Play conducted what later came to be known as the case study method. Le Play's *Les Ouvriers européens* took 25 years of exploration of the European working men (Mogey, 1955). His book was published in 1855 and included case studies of 57 families, each one of them representative of a specific working class. Le Play's approach, which might seem obvious today to anyone with a little knowledge of case study methods, was a breakthrough at that time. It is notable that any strides which case study research has made in the past two centuries is built upon Le Play's labor and methodological invention. Today, even 167 years later, we cannot but marvel at the ingenuity, time, and effort that Le Play put into exploring the lives of the working class firsthand. Since Le Play's days, social sciences have seen a multitude of case studies. From unique cases which opened the doors for investigating some previously unexplored phenomenon to typical cases which helped in reaching generalizable solutions to problems, the nature and scope of case study research nowadays is manifold.

Some remarkable examples of case studies could be found in social sciences. For instance, the (now) popular Phineas Gage is one of the earliest case studies in psychology and neuroscience. In 1848, Phineas Gage, a construction supervisor in Vermont, succumbed to an accident. Gage was preparing the powder charge for blasting a rock and accidentally forced a steel rod into the hole. The resultant explosion pierced his skull and damaged his frontal lobe. Surprisingly, Gage recovered from this injury. However, as his friends opined, "Gage was no longer Gage." His behavior changed completely. From being an even-tempered man, Gage became an antisocial person who would shout expletives and indulge in bad manners and dishonest behavior (Sabbatini, 1997). By observing Gage's behavior and interviewing his acquaintances, Gage's doctor John

Harlow wrote two books on how the frontal lobe plays a role in the decision-making and social cognition of human beings. Contrary to what most sources say on the topic, there has also been some evidence to the fact that Gage eventually recovered from his wayward behavior and was leading a peaceful life (Costandi, 2018). It is difficult to know whether stories about his subsequent life are fact or fiction. Regardless, Phineas Gage's case is the first to point to the role of the brain in human behavior. Gage's case is explored even today by scientists (*Why Brain Scientists are Still Obsessed with the Curious Case of Phineas Gage*, 2017). For instance, in 2012, Van Horn and colleagues compared the CT scans of Gage's skull with the MRI scans of typical brains to further explore the effect of frontal cortex damage on behavioral changes (see Van Horn et al., 2012).

Another example of a popular case study in psychology is that of Genie,[1] a pubescent girl who lived most of her life in social isolation, deprivation, and abuse. She was discovered when she was 13 years old. Genie was emotionally disturbed, uncoordinated, underweight, and could not speak any language. Further investigation revealed that Genie was raised in complete isolation, in a small, closed room where she was often tied to a potty chair. She only wore a cloth harness, which prevented her from handling her feces. She was fed very little food, often in the form of baby food, and was minimally cared for by her mother. Genie never had an opportunity even to watch television, listen to radio, or hear other people talking, since her father was intolerant to any noises. She was punished if she ever made any sounds (Fromkin et al., 1974). The pathological behavior of the family members and the impoverished environment she grew up in led to Genie being alarmingly slow in her development. Genie's case was investigated by researchers in psychology and linguistics to understand the relationship between language and cognition as well as the mental abilities, the stages, and the biological foundations underlying language acquisition and competence (Curtiss et al., 1974). From the neuroscience study of Phineas Gage in the eighteenth century to the more recent linguistic study of Genie, case studies have evidently facilitated understanding regarding different aspects of individual and social behaviors.

Similarly, in the field of political science, Theda Skocpol's (1979) book was highly influential. In the book, she explored the reasons that lead to social revolutions. For this purpose, she conducted a comparative case study. She compared the countries in which a social revolution had happened (France, Russia, and China) with countries in which a social

---

[1] Pseudonym.

revolution had not happened (England, Prussia/Germany, and Japan). To undertake these cross-case comparisons, she applied the classical Mill's methods of difference and agreement which aimed at identifying causal relationships between the variables of interest. This allowed her to identify "causes" that can lead to "social revolution."

Similarly, in the field of sociology, a classical case study is that of Middletown (Lynd & Lynd, 1929, 1937). In their seminal work, the Lynds studied a typical small American city. The Lynds had cleverly anonymized the city that they studied by calling it Middletown, since many places in the United States are called Middletown. Nonetheless, it was eventually found out that the city subject to their analysis was Muncie, a city in Indiana. Regarding the Lynds's seminal work, Sarah Igo's (2007) following book passage captures how deeply the Lynds had immersed themselves into the field, with the goal to understand the city and its residents better:

> In January 1924, the two young investigators and their staff of three research assistants arrived in Muncie, Indiana, or "Middletown." Planting their operation in the city for a good part of two years, the Lynds and their staff attended community meetings and religious services, examined census data and court records, surveyed schoolchildren, interviewed wives, distributed questionnaires, collected family budgets, read local newspapers, compiled statistics, observed townspeople's activities, and lived among their subjects. Determined to reveal not only Muncie's present but its recent past, they read anything they could find from the town's "frontier" days of the 1890s, including diaries, yearbooks, scrapbooks, school examination questions, and minutes of organizations such as the Ministerial Association and the Woman's Club. (Igo, 2007, pp. 35–36)

You could ask why the Lynds wanted to study this particular city. Well, by selecting Muncie, a city that represented the average typical cities in the United States, the Lynds could easily "transfer" insights derived from it to other cities that shared a similar context. Moreover, the Lynds also went on to compare Muncie as it existed during two time periods – before the Great depression (Lynd & Lynd, 1929) and during the Great depression (Lynd & Lynd, 1937). Looking at the same city allowed them to control (i.e. keep constant) contextual factors that were of no theoretical interest to the study in hand. At the same time, it allowed them to identify causal factors that were affecting activities since the commencement of the Great depression.

Last but not least, in the field of management, case study research has been instrumental in providing important groundbreaking insights.

For example, Vaccaro and Palazzo (2015) use a case study to understand how institutional changes could happen in a context that is fraught by organized crime. To understand this, they looked at a movement called *Addiopizzo* that originated in 2004 in Palermo, Sicily. The movement was started by a young activist who wanted to stand up against extortion money (also known as *pizzo*) that was being demanded from Sicilian businesses by the Mafia. Paying the *pizzo* was seen as paying protection money. Similarly, anyone challenging the *pizzo* was considered as challenging the Mafia's sovereignty and often met with three risks – encountering violence (e.g. death), economic losses (e.g. a business being burnt down), and social isolation. It is surprising to see, therefore, that in such a context *Addiopizzo* went on to become one of the most successful anti-Mafia movements. In fact, Vaccaro and Palazzo (2015) indicated that, by 2011, reports on extortion saw an increase, which was unprecedented since in the past people did not report Mafia atrocities out of fear. Moreover, the movement was able to garner significant support by "56 activists, 10,143 consumers, 154 schools, 29 local associations (e.g., the Sicilian branch of Confindustria, the highly influential Confederation of Italian Industry), and more than 700 affiliated firms (over 10% of the entrepreneurs in the Province of Palermo)" (Vaccaro & Palazzo, 2015, p. 1080).

The success of the movement challenged the entrenched belief that nothing can be done about the *pizzo*. Furthermore, this also made for an interesting case to study and understand. Given this pivotal role case studies have been playing in the social sciences, it is important to answer the question – What exactly is a case study?

1.2   Case Study: What Is It?

Robert Yin, the American social scientist known for his extensive work on case study research, defines the case study as an empirical inquiry investigating a contemporary phenomenon in its real-life context (Yin, 2009). In Yin's definition, the case studies investigate phenomena of interest which do not have clear boundaries separating them from the context. Usually, these phenomena involve multiple causal conditions and a relatively lower number of data points. In case study research, phenomena are explored using multiple sources of evidence, with the help of pre-developed theoretical propositions. Since case studies by definition involve small sample sizes, the appropriate selection technique is purposive rather than random. The cases, as well as the participants and data sources, are selected in such a way that they are representative and provide variation along the causal conditions and outcomes which are of interest to the researcher (Gerring, 2007).

In general, a case study is the focused study of a bounded phenomenon through intensive exploration (Gerring, 2004). For instance, if the focus of a particular case study is understanding the eLearning experiences of Master students in a business school, the researcher can select a specific business school providing eLearning facilities for its students as the case. This case could be typical (as was in the Middletown example), as in, similar to other business schools with eLearning facilities. It could also be chosen because of its atypical nature, that is, due to it being an exemplar in providing eLearning facilities (as was in the *Addiopizzo* example). Regardless of the specific reason behind the choice, case selection in case study research always involves careful contemplation of the suitability of a particular case for the study. The reasons behind the choices are often determined by the specific study's research questions and, subsequently, by its designs.

1.3 (Sequencing) Case Study Designs

Yin (2009) suggested four types of case study designs based on the number of cases and sub-cases being investigated. Based on whether a case is single or multiple and embedded or holistic, he proposed the single holistic, multiple holistic, single embedded, and multiple embedded designs. Gerring (2004), on the other hand, provided a covariational typology of case study designs based on the spatial and temporal variations that underlie them. Subsequently, the within-unit (with and without temporal/spatial variation), cross-sectional, time-series cross-sectional, hierarchical, comparative–historical, and hierarchical time-series designs became a part of the case study vocabulary. Blatter and Haverland (2012) added to the conversation on case study designs by suggesting three ways of conducting causal case study research – co-variational analysis, causal–process tracing, and congruence analysis. In this book, we add to the discussions on case study designs by proposing a technique that we call "sequencing case study designs." Traditionally, sequential research designs were introduced to reconcile the use of qualitative and quantitative research methods in the same study (Cameron, 2009). Different authors have discussed sequential designs based on the timing, weighting, and ordering of methodological choices (Cresswell et al., 2003). However, our new proposed design technique (i.e. sequencing case study designs) is novel on two aspects. First, it squarely focuses on qualitative case study designs. Second, this technique incorporates the malleable nature of case study designs by (re)combining the strengths of individual case study designs to suit the unique needs of a research study in hand.

1.4 Purpose of This Book: From Sequencing Case Study Designs to Undertaking a Methodological Tango!

The discussion on case studies and designs brings us to the core purpose of the book. Case study research is a versatile method in that it allows for different data sources (be they qualitative or quantitative) to be combined in the same study. Its main purpose is theory enhancement (theory building and rarely also theory testing). The method has become a mainstay in the social sciences, resulting in a myriad of methodological textbooks and articles, some of which date back to the 1970s (e.g. Campbell, 1975). Despite its popularity, the case study research has been prone to criticism regarding academic rigor and ambiguity (Dubé & Paré, 2003; Gibbert et al., 2008). This book makes four important departures from apparently competing works currently on the market: First, whereas previous case study method books focused on combining data sources within one design, we combine designs and streamline our discussion specifically on designing as opposed to data collection and data analysis. In doing so, we take case study research to the next level by discussing the combinations of different case study designs in the same research study, which we describe as "sequencing case study designs." Our approach is similar to experimental methods in which we find several (typically four-to-six) individual experiments in the same paper, with increasing sophistication and rigor.

In this book, we first provide the essential building blocks of case study research designs. We subsequently discuss archetypical research designs in terms of their strengths and weaknesses, and ultimately proceed to illustrate how these can be fruitfully combined depending on the research question. We discuss the relevant methodological choices on each level, with an eye on maximizing the contribution of the case study for theorizing. We submit that the rigor of the overall series of case studies is greater than the sum of its parts, since combinations of different case study designs embrace different epistemological traditions and cut across rigor criteria. This discussion on case study designs is, hence, the first focal point of this book.

Second, there is a conundrum: case studies are most appropriate in the early stages of theory development, yet often get rejected for the lack of theory in the front end of the paper (despite otherwise rigorous methods). Thus, while its prowess for theory development is unquestioned and in fact touted as the main rationale for case study research, the currently-available books have so far not effectively engaged in the mechanics of crafting and relaying the theoretical contribution cogently to different reviewer camps. We address this conundrum in this book. Third, rather than providing normative prescriptions of what authors should do based on reviews of the methodology literature (as is common in extant methodological books), we provide concrete examples to illustrate both individual case study designs, as well as their combinations. These examples stem from over 30 years of research into case study rigor by the authors, and 15 years of teaching the case study method to students at all levels.

Fourth, given the lack of cohesion in the conventions surrounding case study research (interpretivists describe their research design in totally different ways than, say, those in more positivist traditions), we undertake a methodological tango! That is, we move back and forth between the intricacies of interpretivist and positivist traditions, by highlighting their differences but also similarities. Through this methodological tango, we acknowledge the different traditions but also discuss how dismissing one tradition or the other stating dogmatic reasons might defeat the purpose of case study research (which is developing a better understanding of the phenomenon of interest). We, therefore, choreograph this methodological tango by providing "box inserts" under the heading "But someone told/asked me" throughout the book. In these box inserts, we tease out the intricacies of case studies and their designs. These boxes are designed to make the book more helpful for different audiences – the instructors of case study courses and the researchers interested in conducting case study research. Additionally, we also include box inserts that act as thinking exercises under the name "But before we move on let's think/read/watch." The instructors of case study courses will find these box inserts useful for designing their courses; while practicing researchers will appreciate the box inserts for the concrete guidance on improving their own case study designs.

1.5 Summary of the Chapters

In Chapter 2, we discuss the building blocks of case study research. We discuss the various functions that case study research can play and the resultant types of research questions. The importance of context in case study research is examined afterwards. Furthermore, we introduce the logical reasoning concepts of induction, deduction, and abduction to the readers. In the subsequent chapters, we discuss different case study designs. We begin to do so in Chapter 3, which focuses on the single case study design. The strengths and weaknesses of a single case study design are elaborated upon. In Chapter 4, we discuss the multiple case study designs, with a focus on replication logic. Both literal and theoretical replication are introduced, along with their strengths and weaknesses. The rigor parameters of reliability, internal validity, and external validity are also discussed in this chapter. At the end of the chapter, we also discuss the strengths and limitations of the multiple case study design. In Chapter 5, we discuss single embedded case studies. The levels of analysis and selection rationales underlying single embedded designs are deliberated upon. Longitudinal and cross-sectional single embedded designs are discussed afterwards. The strengths and weaknesses of single embedded designs are discussed at the end of the chapter.

Chapter 6 deals with multiple embedded case study designs. The different levels of analysis and units of analysis as well as within- and between-case replications are discussed in this chapter. We end the chapter with a discussion of the strengths and weaknesses of the designs. In Chapter 7, we discuss the sequencing of inductive–deductive case study research designs. We revisit the topics of research questions, theoretical sampling, controls, and units/levels of analysis in the context of the sequenced designs. The importance of chronology in sequencing designs is discussed last. Chapter 8 deliberates on the deductive–inductive sequencing of research designs. Like in the preceding chapter, we discuss research questions, theoretical sampling, controls, and units/levels of analysis in the context of this type of sequenced research designs next. The importance of additional data collection and transparent reporting is then elaborated upon. We end the chapter with a discussion of deviant cases and the omitted variable bias. Finally, in Chapter 9, we revisit the research paradigms of positivism and interpretivism and subsequently discuss different quality criteria proposed by prior researchers from both paradigmatic camps. We also briefly discuss the iterative cycles of data collection and analysis one would encounter during a qualitative case study research process. We end the chapter and the book by offering a guiding framework for researchers interested in sequencing case study designs.

REFERENCES

Blatter, J. & Haverland, M. (2012). *Designing Case Studies: Explanatory Approaches in Small-N Research*. London: Palgrave Macmillan.

Cameron, R. (2009). A sequential mixed model research design: Design, analytical and display issues. *International Journal of Multiple Research Approaches*, 3(2), 140–152.

Campbell, D. T. (1975). Degrees of freedom and the case study. *Comparative Political Studies*, 8(2), 178–193.

Costandi, M. (2018, February 14). Phineas Gage and the effect of an iron bar through the head on personality. *The Guardian*. Available at: www.theguardian.com/science/blog/2010/nov/05/phineas-gage-head-personality (last accessed July 13, 2022).

Creswell, J. W., Plano Clark, V. L., Gutmann, M. L. & Hanson, W. E. (2003). An expanded typology for classifying mixed methods research into designs. In: A. Tashakkori and C. Teddlie (eds.) *Handbook of Mixed Methods in Social and Behavioral Research*. Thousand Oaks: Sage, 209–240.

Curtiss, S., Fromkin, V., Krashen, S., Rigler, D. & Rigler, M. (1974). The linguistic development of Genie. *Language*, 50(3), 528–554.

Dubé, L. & Paré, G. (2003). Rigor in information systems positivist case research: Current practices, trends, and recommendations. *MIS Quarterly*, 27(4), 597–636.

Fromkin, V., Krashen, S., Curtiss, S., Rigler, D. & Rigler, M. (1974). The development of language in Genie: A case of language acquisition beyond the "critical period." *Brain and Language*, 1(1), 81–107.

Gerring, J. (2004). What is a case study and what is it good for? *American Political Science Review*, 98(2), 341–354.

    (2007). *Case Study Research: Principles and Practices*. Cambridge: Cambridge University Press.

Gibbert, M., Ruigrok, W. & Wicki, B. (2008). What passes as a rigorous case study? *Strategic Management Journal*, 29(13), 1465–1474.

Igo, S. E. (2007). *The Averaged American: Surveys, Citizens, and the Making of a Mass Public*. Boston: Harvard University Press.

Lynd, R. S. & Lynd, H. M. (1929). *Middletown; A Study in Contemporary American Culture*. Orlando: Harcourt Brace.

    (1937). *Middletown in Transition: A Study in Cultural Conflicts*. New York: Harvest.

Mogey, J. M. (1955). The contribution of Frédéric Le Play to family research. *Marriage and Family Living*, 17(4), 310–315.

Sabbatini, R. M. E. (1997). The amazing case of Phineas Gage. *Brain & Mind Magazine*. Available at: https://lecerveau.mcgill.ca/flash/capsules/articles_pdf/phyneas_gage.pdf (last accessed July 13, 2022).

Skocpol, T. (1979). *States and Social Revolutions: A Comparative Analysis of France, Russia and China*. New York: Cambridge University Press.

Vaccaro, A. & Palazzo, G. (2015). Values against violence: Institutional change in societies dominated by organized crime. *Academy of Management Journal*, 58 (4), 1075–1101.

Van Horn, J. D., Irimia, A., Torgerson, C. M., Chambers, M. C., Kikinis, R. & Toga, A. W. (2012). Mapping connectivity damage in the case of Phineas Gage. *PloS One*, 7(5), e37454.

Why Brain Scientists are Still Obsessed with the Curious Case of Phineas Gage. (2017, May 21). Available at: https://choice.npr.org/index.html?origin=https://www.npr.org/sections/health-shots/2017/05/21/528966102/why-brain-scientists-are-still-obsessed-with-the-curious-case-of-phineas-gage (last accessed July 13, 2022).

Yin, R. K. (2009). *Case Study Research: Design and Methods*, Vol. 5. Thousand Oaks: Sage.

CHAPTER 2

Building Blocks of Case Study Research

2.1 Introduction

In April 2019, scientists presented the world with something unprecedented – a picture of a black hole (Drake, 2019). After a long wait, that astronomical entity which mystifies humankind was made visible to the human eye. But it is not the mystical element of black holes that we discuss here. Rather, it is the astronomical enormity that we focus on – the fact that a black hole is an area in space inside which there are gravitational energies of such a magnitude that nothing (i.e. nothing, not even electromagnetic radiation such as light) can escape from inside it.

But how is this interesting for the readers of a case study research book? Well, for starters, the first photograph of a black hole came out around the time Cambridge University Press accepted our proposal for this book. Maybe it is this coincidence which led us to see a connection between case study research and black holes. In particular, the research questions that underlie a case study are very much like black holes. Let us explore this metaphor a bit.

So, a black hole sucks up everything and doesn't let anything out. But where does the hole start, and where does it end? Basically, when does it start and stop sucking in? What are its boundaries? Quite similarly, research questions suck up everything in your study (the theoretical constructs, the data supporting or questioning these constructs, your conclusions, and even your typos). They *are* your paper (or book/monograph). As a result, you often find the research question in the title of a (well-crafted) paper. The research question recurs in the abstract, as does the answer to the research question (aka the proposition or conclusion, more on this later). This chapter is therefore about the black holes of case study research (research questions) and their constituents (involved factors/variables) and boundaries (context).

2.2   Research Questions

The formulation of a research question involves conscious intellectual reasoning. The question we formulate affects every aspect of the qualitative inquiry process from the chosen theoretical constructs to the data being collected, the way in which the analyses are conducted, and ultimately, the conclusions made. No aspect of the research process can escape the gravity of the research question, which makes an ill-formulated question a recipe for disaster. Don't be scared though. A qualitative research question can be revised during the course of the research process. Unlike quantitative research questions, which are fixed even before the research process commences, qualitative research questions are quite flexible. Depending on the data, findings, and the researcher's "reflexivity" (i.e. critical introspection), the research question can be amended while the study is being conducted (Maxwell, 2008).

But before we discuss how to amend a research question, let us first discuss how we formulate a preliminary one. Very much like a black hole, one research question is not like the others. Scientists have discovered four types of black holes, depending on the mechanisms that led to their formation. Likewise, based on the research function they are supposed to fulfill, research questions can also be classified into various categories. In this book, we provide our own take on this, informed by years of experience in undertaking and evaluating qualitative research; and as such we see two main functions underlying case study research questions – exploratory and explanatory.

BUT SOMEONE TOLD ME ...

... THERE ARE MORE THAN TWO FUNCTIONS UNDERLYING RESEARCH QUESTIONS
Various methodologists (see Marshall & Rossman, 2006; Patton, 2002; Ritchie et al., 2013) have expanded this classification to include other categories (e.g. evaluative, generative, observational–relational, emancipatory, descriptive research questions, etc.). But here we stick to the two seminal categories ("exploratory" and "explanatory"). We find this classification parsimonious in nature. Furthermore, one could argue that the umbrella terms "exploration" and "explanation" cover the aforementioned research functions as well.

So, how do these research functions influence our research questions? Before we go down this rabbit (black) hole and explore/explain the difference between explanatory and exploratory research questions, we need to discuss the term "variables." Prior to setting off on a research journey, researchers should have some abstract constructs which capture the ideas or phenomenon they are interested in. For instance, if you are interested in examining how Google addresses gender inequality, you first need to explicate what the variable "gender inequality" means. However, the term "gender inequality," like all variables, is vague and ambiguous. For conducting research, constructs need to be converted into definite, unambiguous, measurable terms. This operationalization results in the creation of measurable entities named "variables." Gender injustice could thus consist of variables such as "share of seats in governmental bodies held by each gender" or "higher education attainment levels."

BUT SOMEONE TOLD ME ...

... THERE ARE NO VARIABLES IN QUALITATIVE RESEARCH

Positivist researchers termed the reasons, causes, antecedents, or drivers of an observed outcome as "independent variables," or their acronyms, the letter "X." Likewise, the outcome of interest is typically referred to as a "dependent variable" or, even shorter, with the letter "Y." Although developed by positivists, this categorization is used by researchers from other philosophical and methodological camps as well.

Nonetheless, several qualitative researchers frown upon such terminology, as a way to underscore their epistemological differences from colleagues in the quantitative tradition, where these labels go unchallenged. For example, some qualitative researchers would prefer to use the terminology of "constructs" as opposed to "variables," as they are seen as distinct terminologies. This is succinctly explained by Bacharach (1989) in the following passage:

> Constructs may be defined as terms which, though not observational either directly or indirectly, may be applied or even defined on the basis of the observables. A variable may be defined as an observable entity which is capable of assuming two or more values. Thus, a construct may be viewed as a broad mental configuration of a given phenomenon, while a variable may be viewed as an operational configuration derived from a construct. (p. 500)

In this book, however, for the sake of convenience and for facilitating the joint understanding of researchers from various camps, we stick to the most common nomenclature – dependent (Y) and independent (X) variables.

2.3 Back to Research Functions and Questions

In Table 2.1 and Figure 2.1, we give an overview of the two fundamentally different types of functions underlying research questions (exploratory and explanatory) and further detail these in terms of variants of each type by discussing how the different types of research questions differ on the "focal" variable(s) of interest (i.e. the independent and/or dependent variable). Finally, Table 2.1 also provides examples of different types of research questions. The first example is based on the Garden of Eden (although we prefer to call it "original research," since for some this is the first "case study" ever conducted, by none other than the first man and woman). The second example is based on more contemporary social science research questions.

2.3.1 Exploratory Research Questions

Let us start off with exploratory research. Exploratory research is often used to identify and display the elements of a phenomenon. Lewis and Clark, for instance, set out to explore (quite literally) a new addition to the fledgling United States (the Louisiana territory) with the declared objective to pinpoint a feasible route across the western half of the continent and to claim a stake in the newly-acquired territory before others got the same idea, along with collecting useful information about flora and fauna and potential economic deals with Native Americans (Buckley, 2021). Like in the Lewis and Clark expedition, exploratory research "maps" the range of dimensions or features exhibited, describes the meanings attached to specific experiences, and defines the constituents of a typology or group. In light of the discussion on variables in the previous sections, one could say that exploratory research aims to describe the variables existing in a setting. These explorations could be X-focused or Y-focused, see Table 2.1 (we explore the different foci more in depth in the forthcoming sections). In fact, even the X and Y differentiation matters less in exploratory research since the declared research purpose is not about finding causality (i.e. explanation).

So how does this relate to our research questions? The general format of an exploratory research question is "What characterizes X/Y?" or "How is X/Y characterized?" Taking an example from the Garden of Eden, one could ask "What was Eve's perception about the apple?" In the contemporary world, in management research one could ask "what are the dimensions of the gender wage gap in Google?" or "what are the different styles of leadership?" From an anthropological point of view, a

Table 2.1 *Different types of research questions*

	Possible types of research questions, based on research functions[1]	Focal variables (dependent, independent)	Examples from the Garden of Eden	Contemporary examples from Social Sciences
Exploratory	What characterizes X/Y? (How is X/Y characterized?)	No causal relationships are claimed in an exploratory study	What were Eve's perceptions about the apple? What were the differences between Adam's and Eve's apple eating behavior?	**Management:** What are the dimensions of the gender wage gap in Google? What are the different styles of leadership? How are different forms of organizational learning characterized, in XYZ industry? How are work dynamics different between Apple and Google? **Anthropology:** How is gender inequality perceived by the residents of Switzerland? **Psycology:** What characterizes depression amongst retired people? **Political Science:** What are the perceptions of young citizens about Brexit? How do world war veterans feel about war?
Explanatory	What is the effect of X on Y? (How does X affect Y? OR Why does X affect Y?)	Both (X & Y centered)	How did the serpent's suggestion (X) lead to Eve's consumption of the apple (Y)? What was the effect of the	**Management:** What is the effect of job satisfaction on employee's productivity in Apple? Why does competitive advantage have an affect on the company's profits?

Explanatory | What causes Y? (Why is Y caused?) | Dependent (Y-centered)

serpent's suggestion (X) on Eve's consumption of the apple (Y)?
Why did Eve follow the serpent's suggestion to eat the apple?

Why did Adam and Eve consume the apple?
What led to Eve's apple consumption?

Anthropology:
How does social media affect national culture?
Psychology:
What is the effect of stress on depression?
How does depression affect memory?
Political Science:
How does the type of political institution affect economic growth?

Management:
What factors make an organization resilient?
Why does organizational resilience emerge in company M?
What factors lead to competitive advantage?
Political Science:
What factors led to the industrial revolution in the United States?
What factors caused Brexit?
Anthropology:
Why is Finland the happiest country in the world?
What factors influence a country's national culture?
Psychology:
Why does depression emerge in teenagers?

Table 2.1 (*cont.*)

Possible types of research questions, based on research functions[1]		Focal variables (dependent, independent)	Examples from the Garden of Eden	Contemporary examples from Social Sciences
Explanatory	What are the effects of X?	Independent (X-centered)	What were the consequences for Adam and Eve after consuming the apple? What was the aftermath of the serpent's actions?	What factors lead to work-related stress? **Management:** What is the impact of diversity and inclusion initatives in an organization? What is the impact of equal pay on gender equality in Google? **Anthropology:** What are the effects of national culture in country A? **Psychology:** What are the effects or consequences of an overactive memory? **Political Science:** What was the effect of the industrial revolution on American society? What are the consequences of Brexit for the United Kingdom?

[1]While we provide possible types of research questions, these questions should not be viewed as an exhaustive list. Instead we advocate for researchers to engage in *imaginative curiosity* to identify "newer" types of research questions.

What characterizes X-Y? (How is X-Y characterized?)

What is the effect of X on Y? (How does X affect Y? OR Why does X affect Y?)

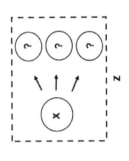

What are the effects of X?

What causes Y? (Why is Y caused?)

Where,

Dependent variable = Y, Independent variable = X, Context = Z.

Direction of relationship = (denoted by) ->, Research objective = (denoted by) ?

Figure 2.1   Pictorial representation of the research objectives discussed in Table 2.1

17

researcher could be interested in exploring different cultural dimensions, with the aim to understand national cultures. In fact, this kind of work has already been undertaken by Dutch psychologist Geert Hofstede, who in his seminal work classified a country's national culture on six dimensions (see Hofstede et al., 2005). Likewise, in psychology, Neisser (1981) explored John Dean's testimony, who was a counsellor to former US president Richard Nixon. Neisser (1981) compared Dean's testimony provided to the Watergate Committee with his recorded conversation transcripts at the White House. As such, this psychological study was important to explore and understand better the "nature of memory." By the same token, an exploratory study could discuss perceptions of young citizens about Brexit, illustrate "how" veterans feel about war, and identify various sustainability initiatives at grassroot level. The common element of all these investigations is comprehension of the social world as it exists ("How") rather than the reasons behind its existence ("Why").

BUT SOMEONE TOLD ME ...

... THAT "WHAT" QUESTIONS COULD ALSO BE EXPLANATORY
Someone is indeed right! However, this depends on the type of "what" question under consideration. For instance, if the "what" question involves identification and description of the elements of a phenomenon (as is the case in our previous example "What are the characteristics of a black hole?"), it fits into the category of exploratory research questions. On the contrary, if the "what" question involves explanation of the said phenomenon (as is the case in the question "What causes a black hole?," it moves from the realm of exploration to causal explanation. In this case, it would be an explanatory research question.

BUT BEFORE WE MOVE ON LET'S THINK ABOUT ...

... YOUR OWN EXPLORATORY RESEARCH QUESTION
You want to explore a phenomenon related to the COVID-19 pandemic. Think and list possible exploratory research questions in the field of management, psychology, anthropology, and political science. Why do you think that the questions you listed are classifiable as exploratory research questions? Justify.

2.3.2 Explanatory Research Questions

Then comes the more popular research function – explanation. Here we move beyond exploring variables and into explaining them. To be even more precise, we aim at explaining the causal relationship between independent variables (X) and the dependent variable (Y). The reasons behind the occurrence of a phenomenon (Y) and the variables that cause it (X) are investigated here. For instance, the factors that underlie a phenomenon, the motivations that led to it, or even the conditions under which it occurs can be explained this way. Table 2.1 illustrates the main formats for explanatory research questions, depending upon the focal variable you are interested in. This focus could be on one or both focal variables.

Specifically, the focus on one variable prompts the researcher to ask questions such as "What causes Y?" or "What are the effects of X?" For example, "What causes gender equality in Google?" or "What are the effects of equal pay in Google?" While both research questions focus on Google, the nature of both research questions diverge fundamentally since the focal variables that the research questions center around are different. In the former research question the Y (i.e. gender equality) is known, and the researcher now seeks to find the X (or Xs) that affects or causes the known Y (i.e. gender equality). On the other hand, the latter research question knows the X (which is equal pay), and the interest is to understand its effect on the unknown Y (or Ys). Therefore, a fundamental difference between the two types of research questions is which of the two (independent variable (X) or dependent variable (Y)) takes center stage in the research, as this will determine the type of research question that a researcher will choose. It is of course also possible that a researcher focuses on both variables (i.e. X and Y). If this is the case, then the research questions would take the format of "what is the effect of X on Y?" or "why/how does X effect Y?" Taking the example of the Garden of Eden story, a researcher could ask "what was the effect of the serpent's suggestion (X) on Eve's apple eating behavior (Y)?" or "how did Eve follow the serpent's suggestion (X) to eat the apple (Y)?" From our contemporary examples one could ask "what are the effects of equal pay (X) on gender equality (Y) in Google?" or "Why/how does equal pay (X) contribute to gender equality (Y) in Google?" We now explain in more detail the difference between Y-centered and X-centered explanatory research questions. Once we explain the difference, we will deliberate on the X and Y centered research questions.

2.3.2.1 Y-Centered Explanatory Research Questions

Often, it is the "why" of the "Y" that interests social scientists. Taking an example from the garden of Eden, one could ask "why did Adam and Eve consume the apple?" Here the Y is the act of consuming the apple, whereas the X (or Xs) are unknown and the researcher seeks to find these factors. From the contemporary world, in the field of management, one could ask "what factors make an organization resilient?," in which the "Y" is "organizational resilience." Or one could also ask "what factors led to the formation of super-successful companies or nation states?" (e.g. in the form of Michael Porter's studies on competitive advantage of firms or countries/ industry clusters (Porter, 2008, 2011) or "what factors led to the Columbia Space Shuttle Disaster?" From the field of political science, the interest could be to unearth factors that led to the industrial revolution (Y). More specifically, the research question could be "what factors led to the industrial revolution in the United States?" Alternatively, a political scientist might be interested in understanding the X (or Xs) that prevented a third world war following the Cuban Missile Crisis (Allison & Zelikow, 1971). From an anthropological angle, a researcher may be intrigued by the recent World Happiness Report 2020 (also covered by the World Economic Forum, see Buchholz, 2021) and may want to understand "why Finland is the happiest country in the world?" Or indeed, from the field of psychology, a researcher may be interested in Phineas Gage, the American railroad construction foreman who survived the accident in which a large iron rod was shot through his head destroying much of his brain's tissue (Siggelkow, 2007). The fact that Phineas Gage survived the accident could make a researcher curious to ask, "how did Phineas Gage survive the accident?" In short, in Y-centered explanatory research questions, the Y (i.e. the dependent variable(s)) is known to the researcher and the interest is to find the factors that lead to the Y. To be more specific the hunt is to find the independent variables (i.e. the X) which center around the known Y.

2.3.2.2 X-Centered Explanatory Research Questions

Another type of explanatory research question is X-centered. Here the X is known and the researcher wants to understand its effect on an unknown set of dependent variable(s) (Y) . Taking an example from the garden of Eden, one can question "what were the consequences for Adam and Eve after consuming the apple?" Here the consumption of the apple is known (i.e. X), while its consequences (i.e. the Y(s)) are unknown. To give an example from the field of management, the interest could be on the topic of diversity and inclusion in workplaces, and their resultant impact. More specifically a plausible research question could be "what is the impact of diversity and inclusion in an organization?" Similarly, a science historian might have an interest in answering the research question "what is the impact of the God particle's (Higgs Boson) discovery on the field of particle physics?" Likewise, a political scientist may want to know the effects of industrial revolution on world politics. For example, in the seminal work on Middletown, the industrial revolution changed the social, economic, and religious makeup of American society (Lynd & Lynd, 1929, 1937). That is, the industrial revolution led to a number of changes which could be observed along a variety of dependent (Y) variables. In a comparable manner, a psychologist might be interested in the effects or consequences of an overactive memory. For instance, Jill Price is one of the few known documented subjects that experienced "overactive memory" (aka hyperthymesia). This condition allowed her to remember mundane details of everyday life, for example what she ate for dinner 20 years ago. A psychologist interested in overactive memory could hence ask "what are the effects of overactive memory on the everyday lives of the concerned people?" In short, in X-centered explanatory research questions, the X (i.e. the independent variable(s)) is known to the researcher and the interest is to find the factors that emerge because of X. To be more specific the hunt is to find the dependent variable(s) (i.e. the Y) which center around the known X.

2.3.2.3 X- and Y-Centered Explanatory Research Questions

Another possible research interest could be in examining the relationship between the X and the Y of a phenomenon. There can be various purposes for using this type of research question, however here a researcher knows both the X and the Y, and the interest is to understand this relationship better. For example, from the garden of Eden one could wonder "How did the serpent's suggestion (X) lead to Eve's consumption of the apple (Y)?" or "What was the effect of the serpent's suggestion (X) on Eve's consumption of the apple (Y)?" Coming back to our contemporary world, a management researcher could be interested in the relationship between "job satisfaction" (X) and "employee's productivity" (Y), or the effect of "competitive advantage" (X) on "company's profit" (Y). Likewise, a political scientist may have an interest in understanding the relationship between the "type of political institutions" (X) and "economic growth" (Y). For example, in their book, "Why Nations Fail?", Robinson and Acemoglu (2012) state that the more inclusive political institutions a country possesses, the more economic growth it will have. Similarly, a psychologist might be interested in "how depression (X) affects memory (Y)?" In short, in an X–Y centered explanatory research question, the X (i.e. the independent variable) and the Y (i.e. the dependent variable) are known to the researcher, and the interest is in revealing the nuances of the relationship between the X and Y in a better manner. One angle this investigation could take is by understanding whether an increase/decrease in X leads to an increase/decrease in Y. Another aspect that might be of interest is to unravel causal pathways, where the X may affect another mediating variable (e.g. L) which in turn affects Y. Or the interest might be to understand the context, which we refer to in this book as Z, but more on that in Section 2.4. Regardless of the specificities, the focal interest of this type of research questions is in the relationship between a known X and a known Y.

BUT SOMEONE TOLD ME …

… THAT QUALITATIVE RESEARCH INVOLVES MORE THAN ONE
RESEARCH QUESTION

Qualitative research usually involves at least one research question. Depending upon the context and topic of interest, the number of research questions could be more than one as well. For instance, some studies involve a main, central research question and several sub-questions. These sub-questions need to be well formulated as they can affect the data collection and data analysis processes (Agee, 2009). Sub-questions therefore are more specific than the main question and should focus on smaller components (i.e. particular variables, be they X or Y) of the topic of interest. This is because the sub-questions can be seen as microscopic lenses which focus on deeper aspects of the phenomenon, for obtaining more clarity. For instance, the question "What causes gender equality in Google?" could have sub-questions such as "What are the perceptions of female Google employees regarding gender equality?," "What are the actions taken by Google management to ensure gender equality?," and "How have unisex facilities contributed to gender equality in Google?"

As you see, it is not necessary to formulate the sub-questions exactly the same way as the main questions. A "What" research question could have "Why" or "How" sub-questions. What is important is to construct the sub-questions in a logical order and in a way that allows them to fit in with the overall scheme of the main research question.

This raises an obvious question – Is it necessary to have more than one research question in a qualitative study? The answer is that it is not compulsory to have multiple research questions. But having sub-questions focusing on different aspects of one central research question would help the researcher in disentangling various nuances of the observed phenomenon.

BUT BEFORE WE MOVE ON LET'S THINK ABOUT . . .

. . . WHAT SUB-TYPE IS YOUR EXPLANATORY RESEARCH QUESTION?
Revisit the set of explanatory questions you have formulated previously (i.e. the questions which aim to explain the COVID-19-related phenomenon). What type of explanatory research questions are these? Justify.

2.4 "Put It in Context": The Influence of Z

It is time for a disclaimer. Unfortunately, social phenomena are not always that "neat." More often than not, more than one variable is at play in a situation. For instance, in the case of explanatory qualitative studies, other variables apart from the independent variable (X) could affect the outcome (Y). This "other" variable could be the context (termed "Z") in which the phenomenon of interest occurs.

So now what is context (Z)? We, like Michailova (2011), define context as the "dynamic array of factors, features, processes or events which have an influence on a phenomenon that is examined" (p. 130). Therefore, the context of a case involves specific details of the setting of the case being studied, such as financial data, business cycle, and organizational structure. For example, let us consider the question "why did the French revolution happen in 1789?" Many contextual factors, such as the political, economic, and social climate of France during that time period contributed to the revolution. But how would an outsider understand these contextual peculiarities? Simple. As a researcher, one has the duty to provide the readers a "thick description" (Geertz, 1973) of the contextual factors at play in a situation.

How do we incorporate Z into our explanatory studies? Explanatory research questions can be specifically formulated to also focus on the context. For instance, one could ask "What causes Y in Z context?," "What are the effects of X in Z context?," or "How does X cause Y in Z context?" To take the contemporary example of Google's gender equality and its causes and consequences, one interesting contextual variable could be the changing nature of the workforce (i.e. the increasing number of post-millennial workers). The comparatively nonstereotypical mentality of post-millennials might be an influential contextual factor that leads to enhanced gender equality.

BUT SOMEONE TOLD ME . . .

. . . THAT CONTEXT IS USED AS A CONTROL IN EXPLANATORY RESEARCH
This is true. Apart from trying to examine the context as a focal variable, context can also be used as a control variable, where the interest is no longer in understanding the context, but in controlling it. Therefore, when the context of a case is not theoretically consequential; it could be used as a means of control. If we choose cases from the same/similar context, which are analogous to each other in all aspects except in terms of the independent (X) and subsequent dependent (Y) variables, the causal effect can be established plausibly. To control for the context, cases should therefore exhibit strong differences with respect to the main independent (X) variables, and corresponding (theoretically motivated) differences on the dependent (Y) variable, but otherwise be as similar as possible. Coming back to our historical example of the French revolution, the historian Alexis de Tocqueville examined the causes that led to the revolution by looking at the period before and after the revolution (de Tocqueville, 1983). By conducting a comparative analysis of two different time periods (i.e. before and after the revolution) for the same case (i.e. France), he was able to control the context.

This controlling and comparing process is also known as Mill's method of difference, which Mill explains:

> If an instance in which the phenomenon under investigation occurs, and an instance in which it does not occur, have every circumstance in common save one, that one occurring in the former; the circumstance in which alone the two instances differ, is the effect, or the cause, or an indispensable part of the cause, of the phenomenon. (Mill, 1875: 452, cited in Blatter & Haverland, 2012: pp. 42–43).

2.5   Induction, Deduction, and Abduction

In research there are three types of "logical reasoning," known as induction, deduction, and abduction. Therefore, a lesson about the building blocks of case study research would not be complete without a discussion about induction, deduction, and abduction. Yes, we know, these aspects are usually discussed at the beginning of the chapter rather than at the end, given that the choice of the research question and methodology often leans on understanding these three aspects. Then why do we discuss them here? One reason for doing so is to ensure that the building blocks of case study research which we discussed in the previous sections are not forced into the formulaic straightjackets of the three terms. We would like our case study enthusiasts to comfortably experiment with their notions and modify their research questions and designs as the study progresses. Yes, this is a "no-way" moment for many strict positivists who would frown upon post-hoc theorizing. But, iteration and modification are the pillars of qualitative research, as long as the research process is relayed transparently to the audience.

Now that we clarified that, what do these three terms mean? As we learned in grad school (or even before), deduction is all about theory testing while induction involves theory building. Pure induction means going into the research field with no prior theoretical concepts in mind and no hypotheses to test (Eisenhardt, 1989; Glaser & Strauss, 1967). However, induction at its purest state is often impossible or, if possible, is impractical. It is impossible to commence a study with absolutely no theoretical notions or hunches in mind. Furthermore, prior theories play a role in narrowing down the investigation process and jointing the case. As Medawar (2013) proclaims, we cannot simply browse over an entire field of study like cows at a pasture. Jointing the case and specifying the focus of an investigation beforehand ensures the study is manageable and gives it a sense of direction.

BUT SOMEONE TOLD ME . . .

... THAT THERE IS NO NEED TO HAVE A PRIOR THEORY (OR TO READ THE LITERATURE) BEFORE BEGINNING THE RESEARCH

Whether to have a theoretical basis prior to conducting a qualitative study or not is an ongoing discussion in the qualitative community. A proponent of having no prior theory (or literature review) is Barney Glaser, who advocates for a more exploratory stance at the outset of the research. He suggests that a researcher should go into the field with no pre-existing theory in mind and no rigid research question. He contends that such an approach will allow the researcher to enter the field with the fewest possible theoretical conceptions,

> and that subsequently this will prevent the data from getting "filtered through and squared with pre-existing hypotheses and biases" (Glaser, 1978, p. 3). As per Glaser, having a theoretical "clean slate" before the commencement of a study will ensure that the data is not forced to fit into the constraints of pre-existing theories. Hence, according to Glaser and his followers, the search for an existing theory (or literature review) should come after and not at the onset of the research study.

Logically, pure deduction means the exact opposite of induction – the researchers go into the research field with pre-conceived ideas and theoretical paradigms which would be foundational for their inquiry. Now what could go wrong with such a structured, neat procedure? The answer is in the question itself. The procedure is too structured and neat to allow theory enhancement. Pure deductive researchers might look for proof regarding whether certain things exist, either find or do not find such proofs, and life moves on. The phenomenon which was unexplored so far will continue to remain an enigma. Now, many researchers have come up with several variations of induction and deduction which would solve these problems. For example, induction is seen as being synonymous to "theory building," in which the theory is built by "moving from specific instances toward general principles" (Sætre & Van de Ven, 2021: p. 685). On the contrary, deduction is a reasoning viewed synonymous to "theory testing," in which the theory is tested by "moving from general principles to specific instances" (Sætre & Van de Ven, 2021: p. 685). Recently, the first author was discussing with a lecturer in her teaching team about how Sherlock Holmes (Doyle, 1960), who claims to "deduce" and solve crimes, is actually an inductive researcher. Holmes goes to a murder site, looks at the clues around, and solves the case. What is it if not induction?! However, the lecturer disagreed. According to him, it is indeed deduction. Holmes has some pre-conceived ideas about what to look for in the murder site. Finding these exact things help him solve the case. So, it is deduction. We went back and forth on this until the first author attended an Academy of Management Discoveries workshop chaired by Prof. Peter A. Bamberger, in which he used the same example of Sherlock Holmes. Guess what, Holmes is doing abductive research! Then suddenly the connections were all clear. Holmes is indeed doing abduction (Umberto & Sebeok, 1988).

Abduction is seen as a form of cognitive reasoning that looks out for new ideas, by focusing on facts that are out of the ordinary or surprising. In Peirce's (1931) own words "it is the idea of putting together what we had never before dreamed of putting together which flashes the new suggestion before our contemplation" (Peirce, 1931: p. 113). Therefore, this form of reasoning is filled with "doubts," "anxiety," and most importantly "informed guessing" (Reichertz, 2014: p. 127). Hence, in contrast to induction and deduction, abduction is seen as "a process of reasoning from data to understanding, with the aim of offering a tentative, "first suggestion" as to the nature of, and perhaps even the mechanism underlying, the observed pattern" (Robinson, 2019: p. 1). Therefore, we see Pierce (1931) in his work positioning abduction as a distinct form of reasoning when compared to induction and deduction. Moreover, Peirce (1931) sees abduction as the initial logical reasoning for a researcher in the initial stages of his/her research, which can change to deduction and then to induction (Åsvoll, 2014; Reichertz, 2014).

BUT SOMEONE TOLD ME ...

... THAT GOING BACK FORTH BETWEEN INDUCTION AND DEDUCTION
IS ABDUCTION

Coming back to Sherlock Holmes, we know that he goes into a field with certain pre-conceived ideas on what to expect (but no real, rigid list of things to find), examine the murder site and look for clues, and finally solve the case. Sherlock Holmes clearly explains to his friend Dr. Watson that for solving his cases "those rules of deduction laid down ... are invaluable to me in practical work" (Doyle, 2021: p. 31). Yet at the same time he does not assert his deduced hypothesis on the case, rather he re-informs them inductively as he collects more and more evidence. Therefore, here we would like to take an abductive approach by revealing our own little "aha" moment, because we feel that the lecturer and the first author could in fact both be right. This is because our friend Holmes might actually be doing both induction and deduction, and we contend that this interplay between induction and deduction can be seen as a type of abduction.

To echo what Parkhe (1993) argues, pure induction and pure deduction are "untenable and unnecessary." Good theory advancement requires a continuous interplay between both induction and deduction, also known as abduction. Of course, abduction is a broad term. The level of induction and deduction involved in abduction will change according to the research objectives. But all in all, scientific development goes through continuous cycles of induction and deduction, which we have tried to illustrate through Figure 2.2. As Figure 2.2 shows, induction begins with collecting the data, analyzing the data, and generating a theory. On the other hand, in deduction, the intention of a researcher is to test the theory. Therefore, the researcher will begin with the theory, collect the data, and then analyze it to see if it corroborates the hypothesis or disproves it. Is it something that no one else has figured out before? Probably not. Hey, we are trying to be abductive here.

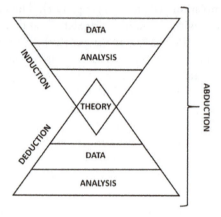

Figure 2.2 Abduction as an interplay between induction and deduction

---

BUT BEFORE WE MOVE ON LET'S THINK ABOUT ...

... WHETHER THIS TED-ED VIDEO DEPICTS INDUCTION, DEDUCTION,
OR ABDUCTION

Watch the TED-Ed video "Earth's Mysterious red glow, explained – Zoe Pierrat." What kind of logical reasoning are the researchers using in this video? Explain and justify.

2.6 We Have Some Designs!

So far, in this chapter we discussed some of the fundamental building blocks of case study research. In the forthcoming chapters, we will see how these building blocks that we discussed play out in milieu of different case study designs. In particular, we will explore how research questions, and focal variables (i.e. the independent and dependent variables) join forces to decide the cases which are studied, the sampling strategies, and the overall research plan. In particular, we offer a portfolio of case study designs which include archetypical designs and atypical designs. We will first discuss the known archetypical designs, namely single holistic (Chapter 3), multiple holistic (Chapter 4), single embedded (Chapter 5), and multiple embedded (Chapter 6). We then discuss "sequencing research designs" that can allow researchers to move beyond these archetypical designs to select a combination of designs that can overcome the weaknesses and leverage the strengths of each individual design. The book in this regard will discuss two atypical designs, namely inductive–deductive (Chapter 7) and deductive–inductive (Chapter 8).

So, hang on, we have some designs on your case study. Pun intended.

REFERENCES

Agee, J. (2009). Developing qualitative research questions: A reflective process. *International Journal of Qualitative Studies in Education*, 22(4), 431–447.

Allison, G. T. & Zelikow, P. (1971). *Essence of Decision: Explaining the Cuban Missile Crisis*. Boston: Little, Brown.

Åsvoll, H. (2014). Abduction, deduction and induction: Can these concepts be used for an understanding of methodological processes in interpretative case studies? *International Journal of Qualitative Studies in Education*, 27(3), 289–307.

Bacharach, S. B. (1989). Organizational theories: Some criteria for evaluation. *Academy of Management Review*, 14(4), 496–515.

Blatter, J. & Haverland, M. (2012). *Designing Case Studies: Explanatory Approaches in Small-N Research*. London: Palgrave Macmillan.

Buchholz, K. (2021). *Scandinavia Is Still the Happiest Region in the World*. [Online]. Available at: www.weforum.org/agenda/2021/05/study-shows-scandinavia-is-still-the-happiest-place-in-the-world/ (last accessed July 13, 2021).

Buckley, J. H. (2021). *Lewis and Clark Expedition*. [Online]. Available at: www.britannica.com/event/Lewis-and-Clark-Expedition (last accessed July 13, 2021).

de Tocqueville, A. (1983). *The Old Regime and the French Revolution*. New York: Anchor Books.

Doyle, A. C. (1960). *The Complete Sherlock Holmes (Vol. 1)*. New York: Doubleday Books.

(2021). *A Study in Scarlet*. Paris: Harrap's.

Drake, N. (2019). *First-Ever Picture of a Black Hole Unveiled*. [Online]. Available at: www.nationalgeographic.com/science/article/first-picture-black-hole-revealed-m87-event-horizon-telescope-astrophysics (last accessed July 13, 2019).

Eisenhardt, K. M. (1989). Building theories from case study research. *Academy of Management Review*, 14(4), 532–550.

Geertz, C. (1973). Thick description: Toward an interpretive theory of culture. In: C. Geertz (ed.) *The Interpretation of Cultures*. New York: Basic Books, 3–32.

Glaser, B. G. (1978). *Theoretical Sensitivity: Advances in the Methodology of Grounded Theory*. California: The Sociology Press.

Glaser, B. & Strauss, A. (1967). *The Discovery of Grounded Theory*. Chicago: Aldine Press.

Hofstede, G., Hofstede, G. J. & Minkov, M. (2005). *Cultures and Organizations: Software of the Mind*, 2nd ed. New York: McGraw-Hill.

Lynd, R. S. & Lynd, H. M. (1929). *Middletown; a Study in Contemporary American Culture*. New York: Harcourt Brace.

(1937). *Middletown in Transition: A Study in Cultural Conflicts*. New York: Harcourt Brace.

Marshall, C. & Rossman, G. B. (2006). *Designing Qualitative Research*. Thousand Oaks: Sage.

Maxwell, J. (2008). Designing a qualitative study. In: L. Bickman & D. J. Rog (eds.) *The SAGE Handbook of Applied Social Research Methods*. London: Sage, 214–253.

Medawar, P. B. (2013). *Induction and Intuition in Scientific Thought*. London: Routledge.

Michailova, S. (2011). Contextualizing in international business research: Why do we need more of it and how can we be better at it? *Scandinavian Journal of Management*, 27(1), 129–139.

Neisser, U. (1981). John Dean's memory: A case study. *Cognition*, 9(1), 1–22.

Parkhe, A. (1993). "Messy" research, methodological predispositions, and theory development in international joint ventures. *Academy of Management Review*, 18(2), 227–268.

Patton, M. Q. (2002). *Qualitative Research & Evaluation Methods*, 3rd ed. Thousand Oaks: Sage.

Peirce, C. S. (1931). *Collected Papers of Charles Sanders Peirce*. Boston: Harvard University Press.

Porter, M. E. (2008). *Competitive Advantage: Creating and Sustaining Superior Performance*. New York: Simon and Schuster.

(2011). *Competitive Advantage of Nations: Creating and Sustaining Superior Performance*. New York: Simon and Schuster.

Reichertz, J. (2014). Induction, deduction and abduction. In: U. Flick (ed.) *The Sage Handbook of Qualitative Data Analysis*. London: Sage, 123–135.

Ritchie, J., Lewis, J., Nicholls, C. M. & Ormston, R. (2013). *Qualitative Research Practice: A Guide for Social Science Students and Researchers*. London: Sage.

Robinson, J. A. & Acemoglu, D. (2012). *Why Nations Fail: The Origins of Power, Prosperity and Poverty*. London: Profile.

Robinson, S. L. (2019). What is a pre-theory paper? Some insights to help you recognize or create a pre-theory paper for AMD. *Academy of Management Discoveries*, 5(1), 1–7.

Sætre, A. S. & Van de Ven, A. H. (2021). Generating theory by abduction. *Academy of Management Review*, 46(4), 684–701.

Siggelkow, N. (2007). Persuasion with case studies. *Academy of Management Journal*, 50(1), 20–24.

Umberto, E. & Sebeok, T. (1988). *The Sign of Three: Dupin, Holmes, Peirce (Advances in Semiotics)*, 1st ed. Indiana: Indiana University Press.

CHAPTER 3

Of Talking Pigs and Black Swans
Single Holistic Case Study Design

You cart a pig into my living room and tell me that it can talk. I say, "Oh really? Show me." You snap with your fingers and the pig starts talking. I say, "Wow, you should write a paper about this." You write up your case report and send it to a journal. What will the reviewers say? Will the reviewers respond with "Interesting, but that's just one pig. Show me a few more and then I might believe you"? I think we would agree that that would be a silly response. A single case can be a very powerful example.

(Siggelkow, 2007: p. 20)

3.1 Introducing the Single Holistic Design

The "single" case is perhaps the best known (though least understood, we reckon) research design. In fact, when we think of case studies what comes to mind is in fact the in-depth investigation of a single case. It is in many ways the simplest (though not simplistic, as we shall see) design. Unfortunately, it is also the most heavily contested research design, as the quote by Siggelkow (2007) foreshadows. Why study only one case?

Case study research, by definition, uses a small number of cases for in-depth study. Exactly how many cases can or should be used and what a "small" number of cases constitutes is very much in the eye of the beholder. Eisenhardt (1989: p. 545), for instance, said that "between 4 and 10 cases usually works well." Gerring provided a less numerical definition and simply pointed out flatly that the dividing line is between "some" and "many" cases. Studying "many" cases using in-depth qualitative methods would be too laborious, "which is why God gave us statistics" (Gerring, 2007: p. 33). Now, the logical minimum when it comes to studying cases is, well ... one case, also known as the "single holistic design." And that is what this chapter is about.

The big advantage of studying only one case is that it maximizes the concentration that the researcher can put on the relationships between abstract explanations (or simply put, between variables) and empirical realities. Unlike in other designs (to be discussed in Chapters 4–8), there is no logical limit to the number of variables we can pour our intellectual energy into. In many ways, the single case study is the most theoretical of all designs. It is so theoretical that it allows for the inclusion of several theories, each with its own set of variables. Paradoxically, it is also the most inductive of all designs since the variables we are interested in need not be postulated ex ante for reasons of case selection.

This brings us to the question, what exactly is a *single* (holistic) case study? The technical definition is "an intensive study of a single unit for the purpose of understanding a larger class of (similar) units" (Gerring, 2004: p. 342). All right, so what does that definition add? It simply substitutes "case" with "unit." This substitution is important, though. As we shall see in Chapter 5, a single case can also have several such "cases" or "units" within the case itself (more commonly called embedded units). Yin (2013) famously called these designs "single embedded" case studies. They are single because they have one case, and they are embedded since there are several (at least two) embedded units or subunits of analysis within the case. For example, a single embedded case study would be the investigation of, say, one organization within which two departments are compared (employee motivation in marketing and finance, for instance), or one nation state with two regions (let's say we study economic prosperity in the north and south of Italy). Contrarily, a single holistic case, which is the focus of this chapter, is when there is only one unit of analysis or case (i.e. only the organization or nation or even a person).

BUT SOMEONE TOLD ME ...

... THAT STUDYING A SINGLE CASE STUDY WITH NO SUBUNITS IS UNSCIENTIFIC!
Well ... as usual that someone is actually right, at least partially. Unless the study of a single event at a single point in time is combined with other design(s), it actually *is* unscientific. Authors of positivist as well as interpretivist persuasions are in full agreement that replication requires an $N > 1$. For example from the positivist camp, Gerring (2007) states that "the evidentiary basis upon which case studies rely is plural, not singular" (p. 27); or as Eisenhardt (1989) states "with fewer than 4 cases, it is often difficult to generate theory with much complexity, and its empirical grounding is likely to be unconvincing, unless the case has several mini-cases within" (p. 545). From the more interpretivist camp, Glaser and Strauss (1967) argue that "saturation can never be attained by studying one incident in one group. What is gained by studying one group is at most the discovery of some basic categories and a few of their properties"

(p. 62). A research design in which there is only one case being studied, without replication among theoretically relevant units of analysis within that case, is "not logically feasible. A single case observed at a single point in time without the addition of within-case observations offers no evidence whatsoever of a causal proposition. In trying to intuit a causal relationship from this snapshot one would be engaging in a truly random operation, since an infinite number of lines might be drawn" (Gerring, 2007: p. 31).

We subscribe fully to all these concerns and still maintain that there is tremendous value in the study of a single case with no embedded units or sub-units. This book is about combining case study designs and, as such, we believe that the value of the single holistic case can only be fully realized in combination with other designs. Exactly how this works is explored in Chapters 7 and 8. For the time being, though, we need to understand as fully as we can what a single holistic case study is and what its intrinsic strengths are. Combining case study designs is about building on their respective strengths while mitigating their weaknesses. Let's explore the strengths of this design first!

3.2 Strengths of the Single Holistic Design

BUT BEFORE WE MOVE ON, LET'S THINK ...

... WHAT ARE THE STRENGTHS OF SINGLE HOLISTIC DESIGN?
Jot these thoughts down on a paper, and then read the subsequent sub-sections for a detailed explanation.

3.2.1 Strength #1: Of Process Studies and Jigsaws

One of the underlying strengths of single case studies is that they can provide a detailed explanation of a process, which (by definition) evolves over time. Therefore, this design leverages the temporal dimension of the case to develop a nuanced understanding of the underlying mechanism of a phenomenon. For instance, if you are interested in understanding how a particular organization has evolved over time or how an event played out in time, you need to examine individual phases of its evolution. The key word in the methodological world here is *process*.[1] In such process studies,

---

[1] Note there are different ways of exploring processes, in different disciplinary fields. For example, in political science, *causal process tracing* is commonly used (Blatter & Haverland, 2012; George & Bennett, 2005), and in the field of management, *process research* (see Langley, 1999) or more recently *process theorizing* (see Cloutier & Langley, 2020) is being used.

we examine temporal phases. By examining these phases, their linkages, and the resultant "comprehensive storylines" (Blatter & Haverland, 2012), the researcher can understand the underlying mechanisms and complex causal interactions (Blatter & Blume, 2008; Blatter & Haverland, 2012; Langley, 1999) which led to a particular outcome.

Single case studies interested in a *process* often rely quite heavily on the individual phases to illustrate the genesis of the phenomenon of interest. Typically, the phases provide the backbone of the narrative and the individual sub-headings of the concerned case study reports are organized in a chronological way, where the beginning and end of the individual phases are motivated by theoretical considerations. In a nutshell, the whole point of a process is to detail the individual elements, or constituents of that process, and in particular how one phase led to another. This last observation is noteworthy, as we shall see.

To give a fictional example, the tracing of processes involved in such studies is quite similar to the one followed by Guy Pearce's character (Leonard Shelby) in the psychological thriller movie "Memento" (*Spoiler alert*, skip to the next paragraph if you don't want the spoilers). Shelby, after an attack by some unknown persons, developed anterograde amnesia and short-term memory loss. The attackers had also raped and murdered his wife. The movie portrays Shelby's attempts at tracing his attackers, with a faulty memory that does not last for more than 15 minutes at a time. The movie shows how Shelby conducts his investigation (which is played in a chronological sequence) and reveals the sequences of causally interdependent scenes involved in the attack in a reverse chronological order. The latter sequence thereby unfolds as a *process*. Similarly, referring to a more non-fictional example in the field of management, Crosina and Pratt (2019) were interested in understanding organizational mourning, that is, how employees of an organization digest their employer's demise. How did researchers study that? By looking into the Lehman Brothers. By thus investigating an organization that experienced "organizational death," they explained organizational mourning as a "process comprised of five interrelated phases, namely: (1) experiencing the death event, (2) remembering the organization, (3) assessing loss, (4) salvaging: evaluate and restore, and (5) creating continuity and detaching." (p. 66).

We are now tempted to illustrate a process visually. We do so by using the fictional example (inspired by a non-fictional character Willie Sutton) of "Why did Bob rob the bank?" Here, as a researcher, you are interested in answering this research question. And indeed, you find yourself in this classical single case study design, where Bob is now your case.

> BUT BEFORE WE MOVE ON, LET'S THINK ABOUT …
>
> … WHAT TYPE OF RESEARCH QUESTION IS "WHY DID BOB ROB THE BANK?'"
> (Unsure about the answer? Refer to Chapter 2.)

You begin by interviewing Bob's family, friends, and whoever knew him. You conduct nine in-depth interviews. You find that Bob had applied for a mortgage from the bank (interviewees 1 and 2). You also find that the bank had declined the mortgage (interviewees 3 and 4). Clearly the temporal directionality of applying for a mortgage and it being declined is clear. But there is more nuance to that. You wonder why the bank declined the mortgage? Therefore, you go to that bank and investigate. You find that Bob didn't qualify because he didn't have a job (interviewee 5). You continue your investigation and follow up on Bob's job loss by talking with your previous interviewees. Eventually, you find a new missing piece of information, which is that Bob's girlfriend had also left him (interviewees 2 and 4). Now you talk to Bob's ex-girlfriend, who tells you that after their breakup she had learnt from mutual friends that Bob had become depressed (interviewee 6). You also ask her when the breakup happened, and you learn that it was around the same time as the mortgage got declined. You now follow up on these mutual friends and two of them tell you that Bob was indeed depressed and was seeking psychological therapy (interviewees 7 and 8). You go to his psychological therapist (let's assume that patient confidentiality is not an issue here), and she confirms that he was depressed and was unable to cope with his depression, and at the same time was also becoming desperate (interviewee 9). You follow up on Bob's close family member, and he confides that Bob told him that he was about to rob a bank, but he thought he was simply joking (interviewee 1).

As this simple fictional example illustrates, the individual (new) pieces of information are really pieces in a big jigsaw (see Figure 3.1). And like pieces in a jigsaw, they are all a bit different. Indeed, the basic shape of the jigsaw pieces and their color could recur depending on where in the jigsaw they are located, but the individual design in the end gives away the exact location of the piece, and coincidentally the contribution of the piece to the overall picture. And, like in a real jigsaw, process studies look odd when even one of the pieces is missing. So, just like in jigsaws, process studies in the single holistic design are passionate about identifying and locating each individual piece in the bigger picture.

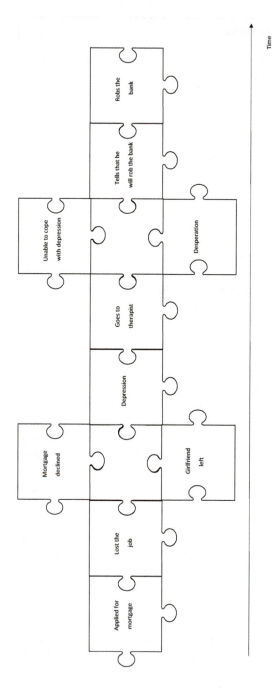

Figure 3.1 A jigsaw process visual of "why" Bob robbed the bank

Applied for mortgage

Lost the job

Mortgage declined

Depression

Goes to therapist

Unable to cope with depression

Girlfriend left

Desperation

Tells that he will rob the bank

Robs the bank

Time

BUT SOMEONE TOLD ME …

... THAT PHASES ARE EMBEDDED UNITS (SUB-UNITS), SO IS THIS EVEN A SINGLE
HOLISTIC DESIGN? ISN'T THIS A SINGLE EMBEDDED DESIGN?

Well, yes and no. A single embedded design, as you will see in Chapter 5, depends on myriads of important decisions. For the single holistic design it is important for "you" as a researcher to determine whether you are interested in saying something about these phases or not. Moreover, it also depends on whether the phases are causally dependent on one another, that is, if one leads to the other, or if they are largely independent. To put this simply, there are no embedded units (or sub-units) within the design if there is no comparison between the different phases. Therefore, if this comparative analysis among phases is missing, and the researcher is only relaying the temporal progression as it unfolded, then you are indeed applying a single holistic design and not a single embedded design. But enough of single-embedded design, we are coming back to this in Chapter 5.

3.2.1.1   *Are You Interested in the Cause or the Outcome?*

So far, we have understood the inner workings of the single-holistic case study. This isn't as easy as it sounds, as the term "single holistic" implies that there isn't really much happening inside the case, since it is holistic, that is, it has no subunits. It is the most phenomenon-centered of all designs. In terms of Table 2.1 from Chapter 2, it is explanatory, because we are explaining the causal process involved in a phenomenon. So which type of explanatory research question does it involve? The answer is it depends on the research objectives. In particular, it depends on the causal direction (whether you are interested in factors that cause the observed outcome or whether you are interested in the effects of that outcome). In the first case, you are treating the phenomenon as a dependent variable, in the second, as an independent variable. Say you are a psychologist interested in teen depression as a dependent variable. Here you would be exploring the factors that lead to teen depression (e.g. bullying, etc.); if you are treating it as an independent variable, you are looking into its effects (e.g. effects on sleep, appetite, etc.). The first variant is Y-centered (precisely because it explains the causes of some prominent/interesting outcome), and the second is X-centered.

Let's discuss the archetypical Y-oriented single case study, which starts off by outlining the importance of the phenomenon of interest (the outcome), often by illustrating how this outcome is meaningful for theory building (sometimes because it is an outlier, or "black swan"), and also discusses how the particular case study provided particularly favorable data access (more about data access in Section 3.2.2). For example, in the field of psychology, a single case study can be undertaken when trying to understand an "abnormal behavior." In fact, Joseph Breuer's and Sigmund Freud's classical work "Studien über Hysterie" (Studies on Hysteria), featured individual case studies conducted to understand the factors that triggered hysteria (Breuer & Freud, 2009). One well known case study was of Anna O (pseudonym that they used) who at some point of her therapy was unable to drink water. Anna O (under hypnosis) recollected a memory of feeling disgust over a "lady-companion" who had allowed her dog to drink water from the glass. Upon recollecting this "repressed memory" and recounting it, she was able to drink water. Consequently, it was interpreted that Anna O's aversion to drinking water was triggered by a repressed memory, which upon recollection and expression of emotion allowed the aversion to go away.

Therefore, the choreography of the exposition for the single holistic design, as we also see in journal articles, typically focuses squarely on the (myriad) jigsaw pieces and how they fit together to form the outcome. This structure tends to be supported by illustrations of the "model" and its constituents (i.e. the outcome or overall jigsaw). We regularly see published papers in which the genesis of the overall jigsaw is illustrated at various levels of completeness. That is, we might see the overall frame of the jigsaw first (the analogy is quite fitting here as also in jigsaws it is easiest to put together the pieces forming the frame). And after that there can be additional pieces/chunks of pieces added; until the final picture in all its splendor emerges. This "pride" in showing off little successes along the way to understand the entire phenomenon is particularly popular in process studies, where the individual illustrations correspond with important phases of the overall process. It is also very effective in providing a kind of visual golden thread connecting the various explanatory factors. These models often look quite fancy and arty, in the sense that there are boxes/ circles in different sizes and shapes connected by various types of arrows (some dotted, some solid, some wiggly, some straight) which go in all sorts of directions (e.g. see the process proposed by Lüscher and Lewis (2008) in the field of management; see Pierson (1996) in the field of political science).

For example, referring to our example from the Garden of Eden, why did Adam eat the apple? Well there are countless possible factors that one could relay, along with many potential processes. One could ask, was it really because of Eve? Or was Eve simply one of the many factors? Or was it because Adam was inherently a curious human being who simply wanted to explore something new? Obviously, sadly, for our example from the Garden of Eden, empirical examination would be "slightly" difficult.

BUT BEFORE WE MOVE ON, LET'S THINK . . .

    . . . OF A FICTIONAL PROCESS OF "WHY DID ADAM EAT THE APPLE?"
Be imaginative, if you want you can rename the characters whichever way you want (e.g., why not Eve & Ava, or Adam & Steve).
  OR
you can create your own fictional process. For this think of a research question, and then formulate a fictional process.
  The end goal of this exercise is that we want you to be *imaginatively creative*!

3.2.2 Strength #2: Black Swans, Uniqueness, and Falsification

Why would one want to study only one case rather than a single embedded case, or indeed multiple cases (see Chapters 4–6)? The answer is quite simple: Sometimes there is only one case. Consider the talking pig in Siggelkow's opening quote. What can you do? If there is only one such pig, why not study it? Methodologists use various terms to denote the characteristics that serve as a rationale to engage in the in-depth study of a single case with no subunits. Cases that are somehow "critical" or "revelatory" are prime candidates. To return to Phineas Gage, the railroad worker who survived the metal-bar accident: There has been only one such incident so far, so we better study it (and we might understand even some wider ramifications that help us treat similar accidents in the future, that is, the study of the single case might help us to generalize the findings across other cases). The famous case study by Allison (1971) on the Cuban missile crisis is another example. Fortunately for humanity, there has only been one Cuban missile crisis, which was eventually resolved, so there was no third world war.

There is a deeper, methodologically (and even philosophically) more profound reason for studying one case with no subunits: even a single case has the power to refute/falsify an existing theory. To grasp the importance of this usage of the single case, let's take a quick look at some philosophy of science. Karl Popper, the Austrian-born philosopher, wrote a short booklet entitled "The logic of scientific discovery" (Popper, 1959). In the book, he argued that scientific progress does not come from proving existing theories, but from disproving them and finding alternative (newer, more progressive) theories. This is where the black swan from the title of this chapter comes in. Say your theory is "all swans are white." Spotting yet another white swan intuitively would appear to prove your theory, right? Wrong! Popper would say, as theories cannot be proven valid (since you never know when someone will spot a black swan), they can only be disproven, that is, they remain valid only until falsified (by spotting that black swan – first seen, by the way, in 1697, on the shore of the Swan River in Australia by the Dutch explorer Willem de Vlamingh).

Popper called this "the problem of induction," to mean that inferring general laws from repeated observations is unscientific and we can logically only disprove (and not prove) our theories. Such cases that deviate from our theoretical expectations, also called "deviant cases" or "outliers," are therefore scientifically relevant and underscore the importance of the single case study. In a nutshell, the occurrence of a single black swan is powerful enough to refute an entire theory of white swans. In the case of the black swans, then, the comparisons we make (and coincidentally, our theoretical contribution) is between the case we have discovered and the prevailing theoretical understanding of similar phenomena. Yin (2013) calls this process of drawing comparisons analytical generalization. This is a kind of misnomer, as it is not about generalization (i.e. external validity) at all. Rather, analytical generalization is about internal validity (i.e. the veracity of the causal relationships identified). If people so far thought that all swans are white, then this is simply proven untrue by the observation of one black swan. *Nota bene* that the comparisons here are between theory and empirical prediction. In this example, it is not our own empirical prediction, but the predictions of others, which have coalesced into the overarching deterministic theory of monochromatic white swans.

3.2.3   Strength #3: Data Access and Construct Validity

This strength hinges on the main criterion for choosing a single case in the first place, namely excellent data access. In single holistic case studies, we regularly find accounts of how fortunate authors were in obtaining data access. Often, at least one of the authors knows certain key individuals in the researched company, for instance, perhaps because she was collaborating with the company in the past as a consultant. While access is important in all the other designs, for single holistic designs it can be used as one of the main reasons for selecting the case (Blatter & Haverland, 2012). As was with the case of Anna O, Joseph Breuer and Sigmund Freud were only able to provide their in-depth interpretation due to "good" access. On the other hand, a complete absence of "access" for our example from the Garden of Eden only leaves us to our own "disciplined imaginative" theorizing which can never provide the necessary empirical evidence needed to support research claims. Therefore, data access can be one of the main strengths of single holistic case studies, mainly because it caters to construct validity.

As we have suggested in some of our own prior work (Gibbert et al., 2008; Gibbert & Ruigrok, 2010), the "construct validity" of a procedure refers to the quality of the conceptualization or operationalization of the relevant concept. Construct validity refers to the extent to which a study investigates what it claims to investigate, that is, to the extent to which a procedure leads to an accurate observation of reality. It has been said that case study researchers sometimes do not develop a well-considered set of measures and that "subjective" judgments are used instead (Yin, 2013). In order to enhance construct validity in case studies, two measures have been suggested by prior researchers. First, researchers have been encouraged to *establish a clear chain of evidence* in order to allow the reader to reconstruct how the researcher went from the initial research questions to the final conclusions (Nair, 2021; Yin, 2013). Second, researchers have sought to *triangulate*, that is, adopt different angles from which to look at the same phenomenon, by using different data collection strategies and different data sources (Denzin & Lincoln, 2011; Jick, 1979; Stake, 1995; Yin, 2013). The three main data sources for case studies are interviews, observations (direct and participant), and archival documents. Triangulation can occur both within data sources (when we compare interviews, for instance) or between data sources (when we compare interviews with documents, as an example). The exercise of triangulation and the coincidental establishment of a clear chain of evidence are key in enhancing construct validity. Triangulation here refers to the systematic comparison of individual data sources with an effort to find out to what extent they all paint the same picture. When slightly different pictures emerge, this means collecting additional data (possibly from different sources) until a coherent picture emerges. However, keep in mind that data triangulation is only one form of triangulation in qualitative research. The other forms include, but are not limited to, methodological triangulation, investigator triangulation, and theoretical triangulation.

3.2.4 Strength #4: Unlimited Number of Variables, if Desired

Single holistic designs can be unashamedly exploratory in nature, if desired. By that we mean that it can unearth and examine multiple variables pertaining to the case in hand. Even when they are explanatory, having only a single case allows the researcher to go in depth and examine an unlimited number of independent variables (causes) and dependent variables (effects) at play in that case. Once again, the research question will provide guidance and bound the scope of the study. Again coming back to Robert K. Yin, a pioneer of case study research, a case study is a research strategy where the variables of interest are far more numerous than the available data points (Yin, 2013).

In fact, single holistic design can accommodate even more variables than you thought of when you first designed the study. According to Yin, case studies are research situations in which the boundaries between the context and the phenomenon are not demarked evidently (Yin, 2013). This seems somehow counterintuitive after what we said about the gravitational forces of the research question in Chapter 2 and that you should be fairly clear with regard to the main variable of interest before you embark on the study. We don't have a crystal ball to foresee the future, however, and when you are actually in the field doing data collection, you might find variables in the context of the case study which you have not thought of when you first designed the study. Some of these empirical leads may be too promising to let go of and so you feature them into the research design.

Therefore, this design allows the consideration of contextual variables, which provides a more nuanced perspective into the phenomenon of interest. As cogently explained by Cappelli and Sherer (1991), context can be seen as the "surroundings associated with phenomena which help to illuminate that phenomena, typically factors associated with units of analysis above those expressly under investigation" (p. 56). In this light, a single holistic case study can be seen as a context-sensitive design. Such sensitivity allows the exploration of the potential variables that seem to float around in the background or context of the study. This provides potentially "powerful" alternative explanations (alternative in the sense that they are in addition to the main independent or dependent variables you first had in mind when you designed the study, or which came up as you were "exploring"). For example, Allison's (1971) in-depth study of the Cuban Missile Crisis allowed him to challenge the "Rational Actor" model, which assumed that governments act rationally. They challenged this assumption by highlighting that if this was the situation then the Soviets would have camouflaged their nuclear sites, which they hadn't done. Through their in-depth contextual analysis of the case, they were able to explain subtleties that the "Rational Actor" model was missing, by proposing two additional models, namely "The Organizational Process" model and "The Governmental Politics" model.

BUT SOMEONE TOLD ME ...

   ... THAT ANALYZING CONTEXT CAN BE CHALLENGING!
Studying the context can indeed be challenging because it is multifaceted in nature (Johns, 2006; Shapiro et al., 2007). However, if you are willing to take on this challenge, it is worth it. As Michailova (2011) points out "context illuminates particularity and specificity while also retaining a certain level of comparability (which) makes it paradoxical, difficult to approach and hence, interesting to study" (p. 131). This means that, while context can provide granularity and highlight unique features of the specific case, paradoxically it can also point us to factors that are comparable with those in other cases. This, therefore, requires careful navigation on the part of the researcher, where s/he can tease out the contextual factors that are granular or "atypical" in nature from the ones that are "typical" or common to other cases or settings.

3.3   Weaknesses of Single Holistic Case Studies

BUT BEFORE WE MOVE ON, LET'S THINK ...

   ... WHAT COULD BE THE WEAKNESSES OF A SINGLE HOLISTIC DESIGN?
Jot these thoughts down on paper, and then read the Sections 3.3.1 and 3.3.2 for a detailed explanation.

3.3.1   Weakness #1: Internal Validity

Notwithstanding its strengths, several methodologists have alerted us to a potential problem with theoretical sampling: Selection bias, in particular selection bias stemming from selecting the dependent variable (Geddes, 1990). Selection bias refers to the situation where a nonrandom selection of cases results in inferences that are not representative of the population. Deliberate selection of cases by the investigator poses the problem of over-representation of cases on one end of the distribution of a key variable, suggesting that a relationship between two variables exists for all the cases, when, in fact, this relationship might only apply to some cases. As a banal example, say you are interested in the factors that lead to ripe, juicy tomatoes (your dependent variable). If you have only one case at your disposal you will pick (quite literally) a ripe, juicy tomato. The problem here is that you assume (and eventually may even be able to demonstrate empirically) that the ripeness and juiciness of your tomato are attributable to several factors (let's say it was planted at the right moment, in the right spot, was watered just enough but not too much, was fertilized, and so on). So, what is the problem here?

The risk of sampling bias in small-N research in general and in single holistic cases in particular is acute when using a criterion for theoretical sampling commonly called "extreme" cases (Eisenhardt, 1989; Glaser & Strauss, 1967; Yin, 2013). "Extreme" cases in this regard are often misunderstood as displaying extremeness on the dependent variable (only). In particular, Eisenhardt's (1989) often-cited suggestion to build on multiple case designs using replication logic to avoid results that are idiosyncratic to a single case might easily be misconstrued. As she notes,

> given the limited number of cases which can usually be studied, it makes sense to choose cases such as extreme situations and polar types in which the process of interest is "transparently observable". Thus, the goal of theoretical sampling is to choose cases which are likely to replicate or extend emergent theory. [This is in contrast to] statistical sampling, where researchers randomly select the sample from the population. In this type of study, the goal of the sampling process is to obtain accurate statistical information about the distributions of variables within the population. (Eisenhardt, 1989: p. 537)

Instead, to ensure internal validity, extremeness should be interpreted in a variational way, that is, with regard to situations where the independent variable and the outcome variable co-vary. The risk of sampling bias is particularly acute when it comes to single holistic case study designs, as the "extreme" case (the particularly ripe, juicy tomato) is not compared to cases sampled purposefully from the other end of that same spectrum (in our case, green inedible tomatoes). Plainly put, it is hardly plausible to establish a causal link between variables (time of planting, watering, fertilizing, and so on) and their outcomes (ripeness, juiciness) across a minimum range of variance (from unripe to ripe, from hard to juicy). The internal validity of such a theory would be minimal, that is, we do not know whether there is or is not a relationship between the variables of interest, and the resulting theory is predictive only with regard to the narrow range characterizing the sample.

The problematic nature of this issue for internal validity cannot be overemphasized, and interpretivists as well as positivists agree on this. To cite key proponents of the former, Glaser and Strauss (1967) suggested that "the adequate theoretical sample is easily judged on the basis of how widely and diversely the analyst chose his groups for saturating categories according to the type of theory he wished to develop" (p. 63). Gerring (2007) states that "the evidentiary basis upon which case studies rely is plural, not singular" (p. 27). A research design where there is only one red and juicy tomato studied, and without any comparison to other tomatoes which vary in their degree of ripeness and juiciness is, as we previously discussed in this chapter, "not logically feasible" (Gerring, 2007: p. 31)

Overall, the single biggest issue of single holistic case studies is that they are particularly vulnerable to the black swan moment; in our example, if your theory relies on the idea that certain variables cause ripeness and juiciness in tomatoes, someone else can come up with an unripe, hard tomato after following the exact same treatment as yours. This is a huge problem indeed, and the single most important (and immitigable) weakness of single holistic case studies.

3.3.2   Weakness #2: External Validity

While the strength of a single holistic case study is that it allows for in-depth and even contextualized understanding of the phenomenon, it is at the end of the day only speaking about one case. In fact, for the single case study (and in particular the single holistic), the issue of "idiosyncrasy" or being too "idiographic" has been highlighted. Hence from this perspective results from the single case can be hard to "generalize" to the population of cases. This generalizability is also known as external validity. However, many qualitative researchers have pointed out that "statistical generalizability" is not the key goal of qualitative research (Eisenhardt et al., 2016; Stake, 1995; Yin, 2013), since the "typical or the average case" may not always be the most informative one (Flyvbjerg, 2006). Therefore, while the case may not be representative of the "population," the researcher can provide "thick" contextual descriptions of the case. This disclosure practice, according to Stake (1995), will allow researchers to assess whether the empirical findings of the case given its context is applicable to another case. This is also known as "naturalistic generalization." Moreover, qualitative researchers have also pointed out that the interest can also be about "analytical generalization" (Yin, 2013) or "theoretical generalization" (Tsang, 2014) where the intent is to "expand and generalize theories" and "not to extrapolate probabilities" (Yin, 2013).

BUT SOMEONE TOLD ME ...

... THAT YOU CAN GENERALIZE FROM A SINGLE CASE!

While the single holistic case can be seen as the "unique" case that undermines generalizability, one can also select the most "typical" case, which would be representative of the population of cases. This thinking is reflected in the "Middletown" case study in which Lynd and Lynd (1929, 1937) studied a typical small American city, with the idea that their understanding of the changes being observed in an average American city will reflect how every other small city in America was changing. Therefore, under this logic the researcher will have to carefully decide what s/he means by a "typical" case, and what characteristics typify a "typical" case. For example, considering the swan analogy, one of the characteristics of a "typical" swan is that it should be white in color. Hence as a researcher you will select a "white swan," as it will be seen as a representative case of the overall swan population (in spite of the few "black swans" in it).

3.4   Brief Summary

Single cases have many strengths, despite their alleged weaknesses. We summarize the main strengths as follows and start our case checklist in Table 3.1.

- The first strength, therefore, is their fine-grained explanatory power (remember our jigsaw example), in particular of phenomena which evolve over time (alias, process studies).
- To fully appreciate the second strength, invoke Popper and the logic of falsification. If indeed Popper is right (as we believe), then a single case (black swan) is enough to conclusively falsify an existing theory, and thereby advance theory by showcasing phenomena that were so far unexplained. The single case in its outlier variant therefore could lead to a theoretical contribution.
- The granularity of insight (first strength) can only be achieve via excellent data access, which constitutes a strength as well as a requirement of single holistic case studies. Moreover, excellent data access could help in achieving construct validity.
- Last-not-least, single cases accommodate a theoretically unlimited number of explanatory variables, or jigsaw pieces. Single holistic cases, more so than any other design, allow for context sensitivity, that is, the inclusion of variables that may not have been part of the original design

Table 3.1 *Checklist table on the strengths and weakness of case study designs*

	Type of Case Study Design	Strengths	Weaknesses
Archetypical case study designs	**Single Holistic**	☐ Fine grained explanatory power (explain a process) ☐ Falsification ☐ Data access and construct validity ☐ Unlimited variables	☐ Internal validity (can't undertake variance analysis) ☐ External validity (can't generalize findings to a population of cases)
	Multiple Holistic	Soon to come in Chapter 4	Soon to come in Chapter 4
	Single Embedded	Soon to come in Chapter 5	Soon to come in Chapter 5
	Multiple Embedded	Soon to come in Chapter 6	Soon to come in Chapter 6

but which turned out to be theoretically consequential in iterative cycles of comparing emerging theory with the actual empirical phenomenon.

Where there is light there is shade, and as such single cases (just like any other research design) come with a number of weaknesses. In particular, two stand out.

- The first and foremost weakness is the lack of internal validity. As explained in this chapter, the single case is vulnerable to challenges from a variational logic. Despite the fine-grained causal paths which it can illustrate via myriad jigsaw pieces, the overall picture may be questioned unless we can show that our findings hold across a minimum range of variance in input and expected output. The bad news is that there is nothing we can do about it. That is indeed bad news, as internal validity is the most important form of validity and methodologists of interpretivist as well as positivist camps are in agreement on this.
- The second weakness is the lacking external validity. Confusingly, this weakness is often seen as the more important one and authors of single cases tend to worry about external validity and not much else (Gibbert et al., 2008). This preoccupation with external validity (at the expense of internal validity) is misplaced and we submit that you should first and foremost worry about internal validity and only secondarily about

external validity. The bottom line here is that external validity is a kind of "nice-to-have" and all you can do is acknowledge it (e.g. in the limitations section) and leave it at that.

REFERENCES

Allison, G. T. (1971). *Essence of Decision: Explaining the Cuban Missile Crisis.* Boston: Little, Brown.

Blatter, J. & Blume, T. (2008). In search of co-variance, causal mechanisms or congruence? Towards a plural understanding of case studies. *Swiss Political Science Review*, 14(2), 315–356.

Blatter, J. & Haverland, M. (2012). *Designing Case Studies: Explanatory Approaches in Small-N Research.* Basingstoke: Palgrave Macmillan.

Breuer, J. & Freud, S. (2009). *Studies on Hysteria.* London: Hachette.

Cappelli, P. & Sherer, P. D. (1991). The missing role of context in OB: The need for a meso-level approach. In: L. Cummings & B. Staw (eds.) *Research in Organizational Behavior.* Greenwich: JAI Press, 55–110.

Cloutier, C. & Langley, A. (2020). What makes a process theoretical contribution? *Organization Theory*, 1(1), 2631787720902473.

Crosina, E. & Pratt, M. G. (2019). Toward a model of organizational mourning: The case of former Lehman Brothers bankers. *Academy of Management Journal*, 62(1), 66–98.

Denzin, N. K. & Lincoln, Y. S. (2011). *The Sage Handbook of Qualitative Research.* Thousand Oaks: Sage.

Eisenhardt, K. M. (1989). Building theories from case study research. *Academy of Management Review*, 14(4), 532–550.

Eisenhardt, K. M., Graebner, M. E. & Sonenshein, S. (2016). Grand challenges and inductive methods: Rigor without rigor mortis. *Academy of Management Journal*, 59(4), 1113–1123.

Flyvbjerg, B. (2006). Five misunderstandings about case-study research. *Qualitative Inquiry*, 12(2), 219–245.

Geddes, B. (1990). How the cases you choose affect the answers you get: Selection bias in comparative politics. *Political Analysis*, 2, 131–150.

George, A. L. & Bennett, A. (2005). *Case Studies and Theory Development in the Social Sciences.* Boston: MIT Press.

Gerring, J. (2004). What is a case study and what is it good for? *American Political Science Review*, 98(2), 341–354.

(2007). *Case Study Research: Principles and Practices.* Cambridge: Cambridge University Press.

Gibbert, M. & Ruigrok, W. (2010). The "what" and "how" of case study rigor: Three strategies based on published work. *Organizational Research Methods*, 13(4), 710–737.

Gibbert, M., Ruigrok, W. & Wicki, B. (2008). What passes as a rigorous case study? *Strategic Management Journal*, 29(13), 1465–1474.

Glaser, B. & Strauss, A. (1967). *The Discovery of Grounded Theory.* Chicago: Aldine Press.

Jick, T. D. (1979). Mixing qualitative and quantitative methods: Triangulation in action. *Administrative Science Quarterly*, 24(4), 602–611.

Johns, G. (2006). The essential impact of context on organizational behavior. *Academy of Management Review*, 31(2), 386–408.

Langley, A. (1999). Strategies for theorizing from process data. *Academy of Management Review*, 24(4), 691–710.

Lüscher, L. S. & Lewis, M. W. (2008). Organizational change and managerial sensemaking: Working through paradox. *Academy of Management Journal*, 51(2), 221–240.

Lynd, R. S. & Lynd, H. M. (1929). *Middletown; a Study in Contemporary American Culture.* New York: Harcourt Brace.
 (1937). *Middletown in Transition: A Study in Cultural Conflicts.* New York: Harcourt Brace.

Michailova, S. (2011). Contextualizing in international business research: Why do we need more of it and how can we be better at it? *Scandinavian Journal of Management*, 27(1), 129–139.

Nair, L. B. (2021). From "Whodunit" to "How": Detective stories and auditability in qualitative business ethics research. *Journal of Business Ethics*, 172(2), 195–209.

Pierson, P. (1996). The path to European integration: A historical institutionalist analysis. *Comparative Political Studies*, 29(2), 123–163.

Popper, K. (1959). *The Logic of Scientific Discovery.* Abingdon-on-Thames: Routledge.

Shapiro, D. L., Von Glinow, M. A. & Xiao, Z. (2007). Toward polycontextually sensitive research methods. *Management and Organization Review*, 3(1), 129–152.

Siggelkow, N. (2007). Persuasion with case studies. *Academy of Management Journal*, 50(1), 20–24.

Stake, R. E. (1995). *The Art of Case Study Research.* Thousand Oaks: Sage.

Tsang, E. W. (2014). Generalizing from research findings: The merits of case studies. *International Journal of Management Reviews*, 16(4), 369–383.

Yin, R. K. (2013). *Case Study Research: Design and Methods.* Thousand Oaks: Sage.

CHAPTER 4

Do It Again
The Evidentiary Basis of Case Studies Is Plural

The evidentiary basis upon which case studies rely is plural, not singular
(Gerring, 2007: p. 27)

4.1 Multiple Case Studies: What Are They? Why Do We Need Them?

Alright, so now that we have a preliminary understanding of how single holistic case study design works, it is about time to make a jump and consider several cases (no worries, we are returning to single case studies again in Chapter 5, where we discuss single-embedded designs). So why are we having this intermezzo on multiple case study designs before finishing our discussion on single case study designs? Wouldn't it be more logical to move right on with single case studies? Well, not really, since the single embedded design includes some features of multiple case studies and, as such, we first need to understand these, with the help of the current chapter.

In the current chapter, we will cover a lot of ground. Multiple case study designs allow for "replication" or "replication logic" (Eisenhardt, 1989; Yin, 2013). In order to understand the (replication) logic of and rationale behind using multiple cases, we need to explore the reasons for which we chose these (and not other) cases in the first place – an action commonly referred to as *theoretical sampling* or purposive sampling. For the purposes of this book, we need to appreciate that, above and beyond the decision to work with several cases, we need to decide between two fundamentally different ways of sampling (or, more simply, analyzing and comparing) them. Yin helpfully provided labels for these two approaches (Yin, 2013). The first is *literal replication* (LR), in which a researcher selects similar cases to corroborate empirical results (more of the same red tomatoes). The second is *theoretical replication* (TR), in which a researcher selects dissimilar cases in order to predict contrasting results (green and red tomatoes).

We will take some time to explore their differences and invoke once more the distinction between internal and external validity, and now also reliability, to underscore their potential. In particular, a multiple case study using TR can remedy the key weakness of the single holistic case study design. Remember the tomato story in Chapter 3? The issue here is one of internal validity. That is, if we only study one red, ripe, juicy tomato and claim that these features are due to the plant being in the right spot, watered appropriately and fertilized with just the right amount of muck, we are very vulnerable indeed to someone coming up with a green, inedible tomato that, incredibly (incredible at least in terms of our theoretical expectations), has undergone exactly the same treatment. To say that this is a huge problem is an understatement. That's where multiple case studies come in. The problem is that multiple cases are confusingly seen mostly in the light of external (not internal) validity since so many case study researchers have been derailed by colleagues asking, "how can you generalize from a sample of one?" Some even claim that multiple cases are good for reliability (see this insert on "someone told me").

BUT SOMEONE TOLD ME . . .

. . . REPLICATION IS MORE ABOUT RELIABILITY THAN VALIDITY

Before discussing this, we need to point out the differences between the replication "logic" used in multiple case designs and the use of "replication" as a safeguard against the absence of random error. Woah! What's that? We already introduced the key criteria of rigorous case study research, internal and external validity. What both have in common is that they are about validity. There is another criterion for rigor, which is not at all about validity, but about reliability. Let's take a moment to peruse these technical terms, which are alliterations as well, making it extra easy to get confused.

Replication refers to the attempt to duplicate the results of a prior study. Technically, replicating research results ensures their reliability. "Reliability" refers to the absence of random (un-systematic) error, whereas "validity" refers to the absence of non-random (or systematic) error in the measurement process. So, what does this mean? Random (or un-systematic) errors are caused randomly, and it is somewhat beyond the control of the researcher. For example, in psychology, a well noted and agreed source of random error is an "unrehearsed response" that is a response that an individual person might be thinking about for the first time. Therefore, an answer on a "gender" question may not result in a large source of random error (due to it being a "rehearsed question") compared to a question on "job satisfaction" (Schmidt & Hunter, 1996). On the other hand, non-random (or systematic) error represents an error that would be repeated or that has a "consistent effect." For example, if you are like one of the authors of this book, you set the watch on your cellphone five minutes fast, so you arrive on time for lectures. We know this all sounds terribly technical, but it is extremely important for ensuring the rigor of any type of research, be it qualitative or quantitative. The difference between the two types of error are also helpful for understanding the important hierarchy between validity and reliability, and even between individual types of validity (we already emphasized that internal validity is far more important than external validity).

Let's start by saying that, without reliability, there can be no validity: A measurement instrument can (somewhat counter-intuitively) give reliable yet invalid measurements (e.g. when you set the watch on your cellphone five minutes fast, the time is reliable but invalid). The point is that you know that the measurement is invalid, and predictably so (over repeated trials). This logic does not work the other way around. To stick to the watch example, you are never quite sure if the time given by an unreliable watch (say, an old mechanical watch, or a sundial during an erratic cloudy day) is valid, precisely because you are never sure if it is reliable. Thus, the absence of random error (reliability) is a precondition for the absence of non-random error (validity). It follows that, first and foremost, we need to worry about reliability if we want to ensure rigorous research.

BUT BEFORE WE MOVE ON, LET'S THINK ABOUT . . .

. . . THE FOLLOWING EXCERPT FROM "A REVIEW: ESTIMATING THE CONCENTRATION OF WEALTH IN AMERICA" BY ERICKSEN (1988)

Read the following excerpt and think about the two questions asked at the end of this box insert.

In 1986, the Joint Economic Committee of the U.S. Congress released a study indicating a sharp increase in the concentration of wealth in America. The committee estimated that the richest .5% of families held 25% of the wealth in 1963; by 1983, this proportion had risen to 35%. These findings came from Surveys of Consumer Finances (SCF) conducted by the University of Michigan Survey Research Center (SRC). The surveys were based on household samples, supplemented by samples of very rich persons selected by the Internal Revenue Service. Shortly after the report was released, the finding for 1983 was found to be in error. One respondent, who had received a very large weight in the analysis, had $200 million of wealth attributed to him when the correct figure was $2 million. When the figure was corrected, the estimated share of wealth held by the richest .5% dropped to 27%. The error was announced shortly after the release of the report, but many commentators had already offered opinions concerning President Reagan's economic policies. (p. 243)

(1) What type of error was committed? Explain and justify.
(2) Why it is important to think through the errors that we are likely to commit in our research?
(3) When do you think these errors are relevant for qualitative case study research? Explain and justify.

BUT SOMEONE ALSO TOLD ME ...

... A DISCUSSION ON VALIDITY AND RELIABILITY IS TOO POSITIVIST!

Well that someone is again right. Again, it is important here to be sensitive to different paradigmatic camps. In our own experience of conducting methodological research, multiple case study designs generally have the tendency to be more positivist in nature. This means that studies with multiple case study designs will assume that there is an "objective reality" that can be objectively captured. At the same time, we do not intend to say that interpretivist folks (that view reality as subjective) cannot use the multiple holistic designs. In fact, we want our readers to be sensitive to the different perspectives out there, and this plurality of perspectives is also one of the key strengths of qualitative case study research (see Welch et al., 2011). Therefore, while for a positivist researcher his/her political ideologies are kept apart from research for maintaining objectivity, for an interpretivist researcher this will not be an issue. However, does this mean that if you are an interpretivist you can do whatever you want? Absolutely not! In fact, as an interpretivist researcher you need to be "reflexive" and practice critical self-awareness throughout the research process. Furthermore, you should disclose your sensemaking process to your research stakeholders transparently (e.g. by disclosing your underlying assumptions and how it interfered in your research). In fact, we would go so far to say that, regardless of your paradigmatic leanings, you should be reflexive. Nonetheless, at the end of the day we want you to be aware of the many different perspectives present in research, and especially in qualitative case study research. As long as you are aware of your leanings and disclose them, you are on the right track!

So, what are we to make of all of this? Our approach in this book is to look beyond the simple fact that we decided to adopt a multiple holistic case design and to carefully decide *which* replication mode (LR or TR) is to be used to (a) select and (b) compare the cases. Unless we make clear decisions regarding the replication mode, we will not be in a position to make meaningful trade-off decisions or further research steps that will guide our overall research process. The importance of distinguishing between the two replication modes cannot be overemphasized as it is fundamental for more complex designs involving embedded units either in one case (Chapter 5) or in several cases (Chapter 6). So, let's start with LR.

4.2   Literal Replication (LR) and Reliability

In order to understand what literal replication is, let's first look at replication itself. Due to its fundamental position in ensuring *reliability*, replication is commonly accepted as a cornerstone of science, in particular natural sciences. In natural sciences, "unit homogeneity" (e.g. all water molecules are the same) allows for easy replication. You may remember the various chemistry experiments in school, in which mixing two hydrogen atoms with an oxygen atom produced a water molecule reliably (i.e. even over repeated trials). In the social sciences, there is unfortunately no such thing as unit homogeneity, since we are studying human beings (rather than atoms or molecules) and human beings, for better or worse, all tend to be different. The results are practically insurmountable problems when it comes to ensuring reliability via replication. In the social sciences (and in qualitative social science field studies in particular) it is practically ("practically" intended in its literal meaning, "in practice") impossible to duplicate the *same* study and achieve the very same results because our cases (or units of analysis) do not exhibit the same characteristics day in day out, in contrast to, say, a water molecule.

Despite the difficulty of carrying out replication of one's results in the social sciences, methodologists have long made influential calls for heeding it at least in principle (Cook & Campbell, 1979). Despite this, replication in the social sciences has recently become a hot topic, following a number of failures to replicate results in economics, psychology, and management, which led to the discovery of forged or fabricated data, with the result of retracted articles, withheld/withdrawn tenure decisions, and the termination of work contracts.

BUT SOMEONE TOLD ME ...

... THAT REPLICABILITY OF ONE'S RESEARCH RESULTS IS NOT ESSENTIAL FOR ALL
RESEARCH, IN PARTICULAR QUALITATIVE (CASE STUDY) RESEARCH!
The dangers of the spillover effect of "replication crisis" to other methods and even other fields have started to gain traction, at least in the field of management. In fact, in management, caution has been highlighted on coupling transparency with increasing replicability for qualitative research. The reason being that while more transparency for increased replication makes

sense for some types of research it may not really work for others, as expressed in the following quote:

> We worry that approaches that link transparency to replication in the pursuit of trustworthiness are spilling over to qualitative research in unhelpful and potentially even dangerous ways. By qualitative research, we mean inductive or abductive scholarship that does not test theory and that produces findings not arrived at by statistical procedures or other means of quantification. This comprises a range of methods including but not limited to ethnography, grounded theory, and narrative analysis. By trustworthiness, we mean the degree to which the reader can assess whether the researchers have been honest in how the research has been carried out and reasonable in the conclusions they make. In a qualitative context, management scholars should be extremely cautious in advocating for the same forms of transparency and replicability that apply in quantitative research. (Pratt et al., 2020: p. 2)

In short, we do agree with the main message of this quote, which is that blanket applications of replication logic without careful think-through should be avoided. However, we also see no harm in using practices from the quantitative field "reflexively" in qualitative research if and only if this kind of thinking is better suited to address a particular research question. Here the key is to be reflexive and to not succumb to research "peer pressure" or what psychologists would term as "group thinking" (i.e. agreeing with others about something when you don't truly believe in it).

So, what does "literal" replication mean here? For our purposes, "literal" replication involves the study of two (or more) cases which share all or at least most of their theoretically-relevant characteristics. Literal replication "ensures" reliability in the sense that we find the same results across various cases which share the same patterns of cause-and-effect. To return to the tomato example, we would find the same result (fertilizer, water, sunny spot, etc. yield red tomatoes) across various trials. Thus, comparing several red tomatoes, all of which received the same treatment, improves the reliability of our findings.

Let's move from tomatoes to organizations and consider the article by Grant (2003) on the strategy-making in the oil majors. The intriguing research question is, what happens to strategy-making (which, by definition, is future-oriented and long-term) if environmental turbulence increases (and, as such, turns any long-term plans we may have cooked up into anachronisms)? Grant's research design involves eight cases, which happen to be the most important (i.e. biggest) oil majors worldwide. Grant managed to interview all strategic planning officers of these companies.

This is really quite impressive, as these people manage billions and are notoriously difficult to convince to spend their precious time talking to academics. In fact, of the originally sampled 10 companies, only 8 responded, but this is nevertheless very good indeed.

In these interviews (which also included other employees in the corporate strategic planning department), Grant asked about the intricate processes (annual planning cycle, individuals involved, methodologies employed, and the content and role of meetings and documents). He went on to inquire about the structure and role of the corporate strategic planning department, and of strategic planning specialists at the business level; including the linkages between strategic planning and the other systems of decision-making, coordination, and control, including capital budgeting, financial control, and human resource management (Grant, 2003: p. 497).

He complemented (i.e. triangulated) interview data with archival material such as company press releases and other relevant research reports and documents. Notably, he also contacted previous managers of these companies which were involved in the strategic planning process. Once this material was collected, he proceeded to draw up individual case studies (one per oil major) and mapped out the strategic planning process that could be observed for each company individually. He shared all these elaborate sketches and illustrations in his published article. He was also very transparent about which companies were collaborative and shared lots of material with him and which ones were less open regarding their internal strategic planning processes. Reporting such difficulties in data collection constitutes a key element in creating the trustworthiness and "authenticity" of the data collection process. Everyone knows that doing field research is not easy. It hardly ever works out as neatly as planned in the beginning and sharing some of the setbacks with the reader is therefore welcome. In fact, this approach of making necessity the mother of rigor by creatively using setbacks and making best use of existing resources is a skill that qualitative researchers should develop (Gibbert & Ruigrok, 2010). So, all of this is good news. After these intricate analyses for each individual case, Grant proceeded to move to the cross-case part of the analysis, basically summarizing the main elements of each company's individual processes into the principal stages across companies (sees figure 1 in the Grant (2003) article for a pictorial depiction of the companies' strategic planning cycles). He calls the result of these efforts the "generic strategic planning cycle" and illustrates it in his paper (see figure 2 in the Grant (2003) article for the pictorial depiction of the generic strategic planning cycle among the oil majors).

Why are we spending so much time on Grant's paper? Because it is an excellent illustration of how replication works out in multiple case studies. Grant specifically emphasized that

> To gain insight into how the different characteristics of a company's planning system interacted and interrelated both with one another or with the other systems of decision making, coordination, and control, I adopted a comparative case study approach. Because my research did not involve hypothesis testing and because the goal was to identify commonalities among companies' strategic planning practices rather than analyze cross-sectional differences, the disadvantages of case study research in limiting the research sample were less critical. (Grant, 2003: p. 496)

So, essentially, his study found the same (with minor differences) strategic planning process at work in the eight companies studied. He confirmed the generic strategic planning process across eight different companies. More technically, he replicated the strategic planning process (the same strategic planning process, that is) in the eight companies he studied.

4.3 Limitations of Literal Replication

LR is not without flaws. Two limitations in particular stand out: One regarding reliability and one regarding validity. The problem with reliability is that the quest for selecting replicable cases is infinite, for a theory remains valid until it is falsified (Popper, 1959), that is, until we find a deviant case (all swans are white until we discover a black one). Popper called this the problem of induction, that is, the impossibility of deriving general laws from repeated observations of the same phenomena (a.k.a. LR). Let us look at the example of the inductivist turkey (what now?) to illustrate our reflection on the limits of repeated observations (i.e. LR) of the same phenomenon.

Russell (1912) was the first philosopher to discuss the experiences of a turkey on Christmas morning. The turkey arrived one morning on a farm. The turkey being a good researcher started taking notes of its feeding times. The first day it was fed at 9 am. The turkey replicated this observation across similar and different days – First day and last day of the week, rainy and sunny days, warm and cold days. Finally, it came to the conclusion that it is "always fed at 9 am." Unfortunately, despite this rigorous data collection and replication, the turkey was wrong. Instead of being fed at 9 am, it was being fed to guests and family on Christmas eve. Thus, observing the same phenomenon even an unlimited number of ways does not allow us to conclusively verify our theory. Popper (1959) insight-fully pointed out that, as such, we can only disprove theories conclusively (via an observation that does not confirm to our theoretical expectations). While this is a somewhat philosophical problem (Popper was a philosopher of science, after all), it illustrates nicely the practical constraints when it comes to LR when the objective is reliability. The message is, "more of the same is not more beneficial when it comes to reliability." Consider the example of Grant's (2003) study on oil majors: The marginal benefit of major oil companies which exhibit evidence of strategic planning despite increased environmental turbulence is approaching zero asymptotically the more such cases are literally replicated. Steely Dan's 70s classic "Do it Again" comes to mind, but maybe only twice ... In other words, in *small-N* research, our considered suggestion is that you can stop replicating after two rounds (in the spirit of The Doors' "Love Me Two Times").

An even bigger problem associated with LR pertains to validity, in particular internal validity. The keyword here is sampling bias. For instance, replicating "literally" several of the same red and juicy tomatoes for comparison does not provide us with a firm understanding of what may cause (or fail to cause) their hue and succulence. If we really want to understand what drives these characteristics of the ripe vegetable (or rather, fruit, for tomatoes are biologically fruits), then we need to choose tomatoes whose hue and succulence vary, that is, we need to apply what Yin calls *theoretical*, rather than literal replication. Unless similar cases from one end of the theoretical spectrum are (a) selected and (b) compared with cases from the other end of the spectrum, the sample might over-represent a single type of cases. Put differently, without comparing cases sampled purposefully from opposite ends of the same spectrum, it is hardly plau-sible to establish a causal link between independent and dependent vari-ables across a minimum range of variance. The internal validity of such a theory would be minimal, as we do not know whether there is or there is not a relationship between the variables of interest, and the resulting theory is predictive only with regard to the narrow range of variance characterizing the sample. The external validity will also suffer simulta-neously since the results may not be representative of the population.

Does that make sense so far? Let us move forward – Your internal validity directly hinges on TR. That is, the theoretical sampling of the cases you study, and the limits to internal validity in LR designs, are basically the same as for single designs (and even the quest for LR's key strength, reliability, is somewhat compromised, as the Turkey example illustrates). Unless you choose (theoretically sample) contrasting cases where the co-variational logic of your theory predicts that a variation in fertilizer, watering, etc. results in a corresponding delta in the degree of redness, it doesn't matter if you look at one or several (as Popper would say, an unlimited number of) cases. In a nutshell, multiple designs fare no better internal validity-wise than their single-design cousins *unless* you sample them theoretically across a minimum degree of variance, that is, practice TR. For case study researchers who are interested in a few (rather than unlimited) numbers of observations, you may want to focus on "extreme" cases which highlight the theoretically-expected dynamics (i.e. those that are particularly ripe and those that are particularly green). In these cases, the causal dynamics are particularly evident (more evident than, say, in cases which are half green and half red).

As we have seen when discussing the weaknesses of single holistic case study designs in Chapter 3, to ensure internal validity, "replication logic" should be interpreted in a co-variational way, that is, with regard to situations where changes in an independent variable correspond to changes in the dependent (outcome) variable. In terms of multiple case designs, this means that, unless we choose tomatoes that have been fertilized, watered, and so on, and compare them with those that were not, we run the risk of sampling bias, which compromises our internal validity. In a nutshell, while literal replication is "nice to have," it doesn't yield much in terms of internal validity.

BUT SOMEONE TOLD ME . . .

. . . THERE IS NO SAMPLING BIAS IN CASE STUDY RESEARCH! (MORE SPECIFICALLY IN MULTIPLE HOLISTIC CASE STUDY DESIGN, GIVEN THAT THIS IS WHAT THIS CHAPTER IS ALL ABOUT)

Most qualitative researchers would highlight that they are interested in "particularization" that is developing an intense and rich understanding of the selected cases or case (Dyer & Wilkins, 1991; Stake, 1995). As such their goal here is no longer to generate internally or externally valid causal claims but to simply explain in detail what is being observed for individual cases in the richness of their individual context. Let's say you get access to two current US supreme court justices out of the nine members. Both supreme court justices you have access to share very similar political ideological stances on major social, economic, and political issues.[1] The fact that you have access to only

---

[1] We got inspiration for this example from Michael Pratt's seminar on "A Bricolage Approach to Conducting Trustworthy Qualitative Research" on November 11, 2021 (also check: www.newscholars.network).

two very similar "case studies" is surely inducing "sampling bias," but most interpretivist researchers would not see that as an issue, because rich detailed accounts of two very similar US supreme court justices have value addition for our scholarly knowledge. While rich contextualized accounts may not point exactly to an independent variable(s) that is affecting and bringing a change in the dependent variable, this contextualized explanation is important and has merits. The foremost being a humble acknowledgement that our world and the human beings that we want to understand are indeed complex. As such, contextualized modes of explanations do not seek out "parsimony," rather they embrace the complexity of causal explanations (Tsoukas, 2017). Consequently the value of contextualized explanations "lies in its different view of how to generate theories about the social world: the rejection of the regularity model of causation, skepticism towards the possibility of meaningful law-like generalizations, and a defence of context as being an essential component of, rather than a hindrance to, explanation" (Welch et al., 2011: p. 755).

4.4   Theoretical Replication (TR) and Internal Validity

As our critique of LR foreshadows, apart from subsequent studies attempting to duplicate a given study's findings, replication can also involve the study of cases where changes in the independent variable correspond to changes in the dependent (outcome) variable. The origins of this approach go back to John Stuart Mill's method of difference, where researchers set out to establish the effect of a specific factor (i.e. independent variable). To establish this effect plausibly, other factors must be controlled for[2] (to ensure that they are similar with regard to factors that we do NOT want to influence our results), so that the difference in dependent variable can be ascribed to a corresponding difference in the selected independent variables.

Let us pause a moment here to explore this idea of controls ("controls" sounds terribly positivist, and interpretivists will cringe at the very thought of controlling anything, but let's for the sake of convenience just stick to that term for now). Basically, as Eisenhardt points out "in theory building from cases, the researcher is trying to, on one hand, control the extraneous variation, and on the other hand, focus attention on the variation of interest" (Gehman et al., 2017: p. 5). The logic is, therefore, to see how a change in the independent variable explains the variance of the

---

[2] Also known as control variables.

dependent variable (Blatter & Haverland, 2012; Langley, 1999). So, how many cases are enough?

TR in case studies is often likened to experimental studies: In a series of experiments, one duplicates the exact theoretical framework of the preceding study and predicts similar results. Notably, TR typically involves designs where cases from both extremes of a theoretical prediction (e.g. good and bad outcomes, or high/low values on an independent variable) are deliberately chosen. The theoretical framework's cogency then depends directly on how compelling the claim is that dependent variables or observed outcomes are caused by the independent variables of interest, rather than other plausible factors (i.e. those that we control for).

In political science, Acemoglu and Robinson (2012), in their book, "Why Nations Fail: The Origins of Power, Prosperity, and Poverty," provide a comparison of two cities, Nogales (Arizona) and Nogales (Sonora), that share the same name, geographical conditions, and even culture. In fact, these cities are only a few feet away from each other. However, the dissimilarities of these cities lie in the fact that Nogales (Sonora) is poorer than Nogales (Arizona) in terms of access to medical, educational, and other services. This begs the question why Nogales (Sonora) is poorer than Nogales (Arizona) in spite of so many similarities? The authors isolate "institutions" as being the main cause. While Nogales (Arizona) has inclusive institutions that benefit all citizens, Nogales (Sonora) has extractive institutions (the opposite of inclusive institutions) which do not work for the benefit of the masses (but for a small group of people). What kind of design are Acemoglu and Robinson (2012) incorporating here? If you think they are using two cases (multiple holistic design) with TR, you are right!

Similarly, to explain TR in psychology, we would like to use twin studies to investigate the nurture–nature debate. While these studies have largely been dominated by quantitative research, we will try to explain this in the context of multiple holistic case study design using TR. Our intention is to make you familiar with the thought process, and to show how it might look in the field of psychology. The nurture–nature debate is highly contested (e.g. see the *New York Times* article by Brody (2018); see also the *Guardian* article by Anthony (2018)), where on one hand "nurture" proponents attribute human behavior to environmental causes and on the other hand "nature" proponents attribute it to one's genes. One way to explain this better might be to study two identical twins, and study them in two separate households (e.g., due to the divorce of parents). Given that their genes are the same, any differences in their behavior can be attributed to different household environments. In fact, the 1998 movie "The Parent Trap" showcases this very explicitly, (*SPOILER ALERT* skip to the next paragraph to avoid any spoilers) in which a divorced couple who separate after their identical twin daughters' birth (Hallie & Annie) decide to bring them up separately on their own without the twins ever meeting each other.

One can only imagine the horror and the shock that the twins must have experienced when they get reunited by pure coincidence at a summer camp. However, there were visible differences between the twins. For one thing, Hallie, brought up in Napa Valley (California, US), and Annie, brought up in London (England), had different English accents (i.e. one American and the other British). But, more importantly, there were behavioral differences too. For example, Hallie was meaner than Annie (if you have watched the movie you would probably agree). Then this begs the question, where does this behavioral difference arise from? If you think like psychologist Oliver James, you will probably make this a case for the nurture explanation (also see his article in *The Guardian*, James, 2016). You would probably contend that Hallie, having lived with her father in the US, was exposed to a different set of environmental conditions than Annie, who was brought up by her mother in the UK.

Likewise, in management, TR was done by Schweizer (2005) who was interested in the nature of mergers and acquisitions by explaining "how a biotech company is integrated into a pharmaceutical company seeking access to the biotech company's know-how, technologies, and innovative capabilities" (p. 1051). Schweizer (2005) goes on to justify the selection of his multiple cases through the following quote:

> When analyzing a rather small sample of cases such as this one, "extreme" research sites, also called "polar types," should be chosen. Thus, this sample includes not only successful deals like Pharmacia-Sugen, but also failed deals such as the acquisitions of Genetic Therapy and SyStemix by Novartis. (This attribution of failure is based on the divestment of SyStemix, i.e., the subsequent consolidation of SyStemix with Genetic Therapy, and evaluations provided during my interviews with managers from both sides.) The comparability of the cases was enhanced by two further features of the sample: in each target and bidder pair, the two firms had similar origins, and the size difference between target and bidder was similar across all the cases. (p. 1055)

This quote beautifully explains how selections of multiple cases using a TR logic was done.

BUT BEFORE WE MOVE ON, LET'S THINK ABOUT ...

... THE THREE TR EXAMPLES ILLUSTRATED ABOVE

Example #1: Nogales (Arizona) and Nogales (Sonora)

(1) What are the independent, dependent, and control variables here for the two cases?

Example #2: The Parent Trap (can skip if you haven't watched the movie)

(1) How many cases do you have here? Indicate the names of these cases explicitly.
(2) Which independent, dependent and control variables will you investigate? Explain and justify.
(3) Do you think the selected cases are enough given the independent and dependent variables you are investigating? Explain and justify (more to come on this subject in Section 4.6).

Example #3: Mergers and acquisitions

(1) Why do you think Schweizer (2005) is advocating for "'extreme' research sites, also called 'polar types'" (p. 1055) when dealing with a small number of cases?
(2) How does Schweizer (2005) enhance comparability among the selected cases? Why do you think this is important?
(3) Factors that are comparable across cases can be classified as what type of variable?

Cook and Campbell (1979) were the first to coin the widely accepted term of "internal validity" to refer to such covariational relationships between independent variables and outcomes. Cases should therefore exhibit strong differences with respect to the main independent variables, corresponding differences on the dependent variable or outcome variable (ideally, these should be theoretically predicted), and otherwise be as similar as possible. John Stuart Mill pointed out that "we can either find an instance in nature suited to our purpose, or, by artificial arrangement of circumstances make one" (Mill, 1875: p. 249). Since case study research by definition precludes manipulation, the emphasis here is on "finding" the right cases (i.e. those that exhibit the characteristics necessary to make causal claims). The characteristics of the selected cases then directly determine the possibility of the case researcher to make internally valid conclusions, which is why cases need to be sampled theoretically (i.e. so that their characteristics allow for a test of a causal argument, focusing on the variables of theoretical interest, while keeping others constant, or "controlled"). As such, TR is all about "finding" the "right" cases non-probabilistically (through theoretical sampling) and ensuring internal validity.

BUT SOMEONE TOLD ME ...

... MULTIPLE CASES ARE ALL ABOUT GENERALIZABILITY[3] AND NOT INTERNAL VALIDITY

We have to (partially) disagree with "someone" here. By "partially" we mean that multiple cases using TR primarily afford internal validity, and as a side-effect enhance also external validity (we discuss this in the subsequent section). But let's take things step-by-step.

Generalizability or external validity is not the only quality criterion for gauging the rigor of research procedures, nor is it the most important one. Yet, when it comes to case study[4] research, most disclaimers refer only to their (limited) generalizability. For instance, in a survey spanning 20 years of management case study research, one of the authors of this book found that researchers worried mostly about external rather than internal validity (see Gibbert et al., 2008). In particular, these articles referred to "statistical generalizability" where "an inference is made about a population [...] on the basis of empirical data collected about a sample" (Yin, 2003: pp. 32–33).

According to Tsang and Williams (2012), "statistical generalizability" can be either within or across populations. Within-population generalizability refers to the degree to which findings can be applied to the corresponding population. In contrast, cross-population generalizability refers to the extent to which findings from one sample in one population might be applicable to other populations existing in similar contexts and periods of time. Cross-population generalizability can further be detailed into temporal and contextual generalizability, with the former referring to generalizability across populations in different contexts with similar time periods, and the latter with different time periods but similar contexts (Tsang & Williams, 2012).

---

[3] We use the terms "external validity" and "generalizability" interchangeably in this book.

[4] As is customary, this book uses "case study research" and qualitative research interchangeably. Irrespective of whether positivist or interpretivist interpretations are used, both are concerned with deep analysis of a few carefully delineated units of analysis with the purpose of explaining a certain phenomenon.

Surely with the best of intentions to help practicing case study researchers who have given or attended seminars and were derailed by colleagues preoccupied with one or more types of statistical generalizability, methodologists have focused narrowly on replication logic as a remedy for statistical generalizability issues. Replication logic therefore was unfortunately not put in the context of other, more important forms of validity, in particular internal validity. The unfortunate result is myriad types of generalizability (too many to list efficiently), with fuzzy boundary conditions, varying degrees of applicability to qualitative research, and unclear connections with other forms of validity (for a review in management, see Tsang & Williams, 2012). Why do qualitative case study researchers worry so much about generalizability then?

Lacking precision when it comes to which kind of replication logic is used

Case studies by definition use a small sample size consisting of only one or a few cases (March et al., 1991), so it is only natural for authors to problematize whether their results are idiosyncratic to the case at hand or are generalizable beyond the studied case. Yin (1981), and later Eisenhardt (1989), launched very influential calls for research designs involving multiple cases, for theory building and for external validity (Eisenhardt, 1989; Yin, 2013). In these influential calls, it was argued that multiple cases following a "replication logic" enable comparisons and as such enhance external validity.

However, despite this common usage of *replication logic* in ensuring statistical generalizability, researchers often do not distinguish between LR and TR logics. While LR helps us in ensuring reliability, TR's *foremost* contribution is ensuring internal validity (Cook & Campbell, 1979; Mill, 1875). TR helps researchers to be confident about the *internal* validity (i.e. independent variables and their relationship with the dependent variables in the studied sample). The point is that, unless researchers have this confidence in the causal relationships in their sample, there is little point in worrying about the generalizability of these findings beyond (i.e. "external" to) that sample (Cook & Campbell, 1979).

The researchers therefore conduct theoretical sampling, that is, "select cases which are particularly suitable for illuminating and extending relationships among constructs" (Eisenhardt & Graebner, 2007: p. 27). The commonly-used analogy is from experimental research, where individual experiments are also not "sampled" randomly from a population of experiments but are rather chosen for their propensity to offer theoretical insight, often in a series of experiments. In such experiments, certain variables and their relationships are replicated and others are added to the base design so as to achieve more plausible relationships between variables, exclude confounding variables, and ultimately generate more internally valid theory (see Yin, 2003; see also Glaser & Strauss, 1967). Despite this, the majority of the authors in the 20-year

> study that we cited previously (see the beginning of this box insert) discussed (statistical) generalizability rather than the far more important criterion of internal validity (Gibbert et al., 2008).
>
> Overall, then, there have been misguided calls for using multiple cases predominantly to ensure external validity. Mind you, there is nothing wrong with external validity per se, but the problem is that these calls for external validity have somehow tended to out-crowd the far more important criterion of internal validity. In using multiple cases, we need to get our priorities right, that is, focus first and foremost on internal validity. Once you get that sorted out, external validity almost automatically follows, as we will now explain.

4.5   Theoretical Replication (TR) and External Validity

As the previous box insert shows, once internal validity is ensured (and only then), we can focus on using (theoretical) replication logic to enhance external validity. External validity is grounded in the intuitive belief that theories must be shown to account for phenomena not only in the setting in which they are studied, but also in other settings (see Calder et al., 1982; McGrath & Brinberg, 1983). We said, in the beginning of that box, that external validity is a kind of "side-product" of TR. How does this work? Very simple! Empirical findings based on TR will stipulate both how cases are different as well as how they are similar (which represent the very criteria underlying the case selection). Notably, by explicitly spelling out the theoretical rationale for selecting cases, by definition, we also spell out how representative they are of other, unexplored cases. That is, we coincidentally also spell out their relevance outside the studied sample, a.k.a. external validity.

In principle, therefore, generalizing from case study research follows the same logic as generalizing from large-N research, which is why "it makes sense to speak of 'statistical generalization'" when it comes to characterizing generalizability of case studies (Blatter & Haverland, 2012: p. 69). Large-N research, by virtue of using random sampling, logically has a wider generalizability (since it controls for a theoretically infinite number of alternative explanations without explicitly specifying them). Case study research on the other hand can plausibly only be generalized to unstudied cases as long as they correspond to the studied cases in terms of the control variables, and the range of variation in terms of theoretically relevant factors. Thus, the generalizability of case studies relative to large-N research is a matter of *degree*, not a matter of *kind*.

BUT SOMEONE TOLD ME ...

... THAT "STATISTICAL GENERALIZATION" IS NOT THE GOAL OF QUALITATIVE MULTIPLE CASE STUDIES, IN FACT IT IS THEORETICAL GENERALIZATION!

Over the past five decades, authors of various epistemological persuasions (see Glaser & Strauss, 1967; Lee & Baskerville, 2003; Tsang & Williams, 2012; Yin, 2013) have fervently argued that different *types* of generalizability apply to case studies and quantitative research. A case in point is Yin, who stresses on several occasions that "a fatal flaw in doing case studies is to conceive of statistical generalization as the method of generalizing results of a case study" (Yin, 2003: p. 32). In particular, Yin (2013) distinguishes "statistical generalization" from "analytical generalization." Analytical generalization refers to the following situation, where "the investigator is striving to generalize a particular set of results to some broader theory. [...] The generalization is not automatic, however. A theory must be tested by replicating the findings in a second or third [setting] where the theory has specified the same result should occur" (Yin, 2003: p. 37).

The correct mode of generalization to utilize in case studies for some is, therefore, not statistical generalization, but analytic generalization, also known as theoretical generalization (Tsang & Williams, 2012).

BUT SOMEONE TOLD ME ...

... THAT ANALYTICAL GENERALIZATION IS ABOUT LITERAL REPLICATION!

It must be appreciated that Yin (2013) uses analytic generalization and replication almost interchangeably: "analytic generalization, in which a previously developed theory is used as a template with which to compare the empirical results of the case study. If two or more cases are shown to support the same theory, replication can be claimed" (Yin, 2003: pp. 32–33).

As can be seen from carefully perusing these quotes, "analytical generalization" as Yin conceptualizes is about LR, rather than the applicability or validity of the uncovered relationships beyond the immediate case(s) studied. Yin, thus, actively dismisses the usual interpretation of "statistical generalization" as an appropriate methodological criterion for case studies, Instead, he refers squarely to the reliability of the research findings across repeated trials. Plainly put, analytical generalization is about LR, rather than external validity.

BUT SOMEONE ALSO TOLD ME …

… THAT GENERALIZABILITY SHOULD NOT EVEN BE A CRITERION TO EVALUATE
QUALITATIVE MULTIPLE CASE STUDIES!

Many qualitative researchers here would argue that there are many factors that are in fact unique or particular to that set of cases. Indeed "local conditions, in short, make it impossible to generalize. If there is a 'true' generalization, it is that there can be no generalization" (Lincoln & Guba, 1985: p. 124). Hence the term "generalization" is seen as a misnomer for qualitative research and for some "transferability" is seen as the more appropriate term (Lincoln & Guba, 1985). Transferability allows a researcher to make the call regarding the extent to which context A of case A is similar to context B of case B. If the contexts are congruent, then you may "transfer" theoretical understandings from case A to case B. Others would see "particularization" as the more appropriate term. As Stake (1995) explains: "The real business of case study is particularization, not generalization. We take a particular case and come to know it well not primarily as to how it is different from others but what it is, what it does. There is emphasis on uniqueness" (p. 7).

4.6 Limitations of Theoretical Replication

So far it almost looks like we are advocating TR over LR when it comes to selecting a replication logic for multiple cases. That is only partly true. In the end, this book is about empowering you as an empirical, qualitative researcher to make more informed choices when it comes to case study designs. To make such choices, we need to also appreciate the limitations of TR. The biggest limitation is that TR accommodates only a limited number of explanatory variables. It shares this limitation with experimental research (so-called factorial designs). To begin with, if you want to see the effect of fertilizer on tomato growth, you need at least two plants, right? Those that are fertilized and those that are not. If you extend the design by a second factor (water, watered or not watered), you need four plants, that is, the logical intersections of crossing the two factors in a 2 × 2 design. Let's say you are interested in a more fine-grained variance of one of the explanatory factors and administer three different levels of fertilizer (no fertilizer, a medium amount, and a full amount), with the second factor being water (i.e. watered or not watered). Then you end up with a 2 × 3 design = 6 different combinations, all of which require a corresponding observation – that is, six cases.

But some might say, do we really need all possible combinations? The answer is "yes," since failure to study even one case leaves you with an "indeterminate research design," that is you are not observing all possible combinations. In qualitative research, this process of observing all possible combinations often leads one to "theoretical saturation." Glaser and Strauss (1967) provide a straightforward definition of theoretical saturation as when additional data no longer provides any new theoretical insights (Glaser & Strauss, 1967), hence our "Love Me Two Times" recommendation when it comes to LR. In small-N research, it makes little sense to keep on replicating the same thing over and over again. Recall also that the quest for saturation – and by implication the need to study yet another case – is infinite, for a theory remains valid until it is falsified (Popper, 1959). So, adding a third replication yields very little indeed (in case studies – the story might be different in romantic relationships).

So how many cases do we need to reach theoretical saturation in TR? It depends on your research design! Let's throw in a third explanatory variable (say, temperature) and keep (for simplicity) all three factors on two levels. You end up with a $2 \times 2 \times 2$ (or 2^3) design which yields eight different combinations of multiple cases that you need to find. Can you see where we are going here? Every additional independent variable (explanatory variable) increases the complexity of your research design exponentially. If you added a fourth variable again on two levels, you end up with 16 cases (i.e. 2^4). The problem is first finding and then analyzing (all) these cases, since, in multiple holistic case study design, you are not manipulating conditions as experimental researchers do. Rather, you need to "find" cases that exhibit these characteristics (a.k.a. theoretical sample), and subsequently analyze them in depth. While this seems feasible for "a few" cases, it becomes increasingly difficult for "many" cases.

Eisenhardt (1989) provided much-needed practical guidance by suggesting that "a number of 4–10 cases usually works well" (Eisenhardt, 1989: p. 545). Each case thus stands on its own as an independent unit of analysis. She further goes on to say that, with fewer than four cases, it may be difficult to generate a theory with much depth and its theoretical grounding remains unconvincing, whereas with more than 10 cases the marginal benefit of adding yet another replication is outweighed by having to cope with the complexity and volume of the data (Eisenhardt, 1989). Eisenhardt's admonition to generate theory with "enough depth" simply refers to the number of explanatory factors. One factor (requiring two cases) may be a bit lean, and (according to her) two is about right (yielding a sample of four cases), or even three (yielding eight cases).

BUT BEFORE WE MOVE ON, LET'S THINK ...

... ABOUT EISENHARDT'S (1989) FOLLOWING (FAMOUS) QUOTE:
Finally, while there is no ideal number of cases, a number between
4 and 10 cases usually works well. With fewer than 4 cases, it is often
difficult to generate theory with much complexity, and its empirical
grounding is likely to be unconvincing, unless the case has several mini-
cases within it. (p. 545)

Against our discussion of LR and TR,

(1) How does Eisenhardt's recommendation mix up TR and LR?
(2) For two explanatory factors, you need four cases (2^2) (assuming two
levels per case, e.g. high and low), for three factors you need eight (2^3).
So where do the other two cases come from since she is advocating for
4 to 10 cases? Explain.

Gerring (2007) observes that the very rationale of case studies is to
analyze a few cases in depth (qualitatively) and points out that beyond a
certain (small) number of cases, "in order to reach meaningful conclusions
about [such a] pile of data, it will be necessary to reduce informational
overload, which is why God gave us statistics" (Gerring, 2007: p. 33). In
other words, whereas it is logically impossible to stipulate with certainty
how many replications are needed to reach theoretical saturation in the
case of LR, TR logically requires at least two cases for each factor.

4.7 Strengths and Weaknesses

4.7.1 Strength #1: Literal Replication and Reliability

Repeated observations of the same phenomenon is what we need (at least
in theory) to ensure the most fundamental rigor criterion, namely reliability. The message here is if you can replicate, by all means, do replicate.
"Do it again" if you can, but don't overdo it, that is, two replications will
be sufficient, in our considered opinion.

4.7.2 Strength #2: Theoretical Replication and Internal Validity

TR represents a tool first and foremost for enhancing the possibility of
making causal claims. That is, it enhances internal validity in terms of
theoretical sampling, which means nothing else than controlling for some

variables, while explicitly mentioning the focal dependent and independent variables. Replication logic is based on the method of difference, which sets out to compare cases which are comparable with regard to plausible alternative explanations but differ with regard to the independent variables of interest which are believed to cause the observed effects on the dependent variable(s). We suggest that these desirable characteristics of case studies be spelled out ex ante, so readers can appreciate the rationale for case selection and the cogency of the causal argument.

4.7.3 Strength #3: The Side Product of Internal Validity, that is, External Validity

Practicing TR logically requires spelling out the characteristics of the cases we chose during theoretical sampling. That is, we outline the explanatory factors and how they vary. We also discuss what makes them similar in terms of those variables which we do not want to influence the results, that is, which are outside of our theoretical framework. The good news is that, in doing so, we describe the characteristics of these cases in depth, which, by definition, also spells out how representative they are of other, unstudied cases. That is, we coincidentally also spell out their relevance outside the studied sample, a.k.a. their external validity.

4.7.4 Weakness #1: Depth of Observation vs. Breadth

Discussions on the depth vs breadth topic famously go back, at least in the field of management, to the "better stories" versus "better constructs" debate (Dyer & Wilkins, 1991; Eisenhardt, 1989, 1991). Dyer and Wilkins (1991) pushes for "depth" in case study analysis and would even see value in studying the single case. This is because even one case can provide unique in-depth insights, and as such Dyer and Wilkins's (1991) call for "better stories." They go on to say that Eisenhardt's (1989) paper, which also advocates for multiple cases, is in fact focusing on "better constructs" that focus on patterns and regularities. As evident from this, the issue between Dyer and Wilkins's (1991) and Eisenhardt's (1989, 1991) take on case study design is more about whether you want to focus on the depth of observations or on the breadth of observations. One can also see parallels between this debate and the debate between particularization versus generalization, which we have discussed previously. Therefore, with a multiple holistic case study design, as a researcher you are likely to compromise on the depth of your explanation, because the purpose of a multiple holistic design is to compare either similarities, differences, or both. At the end of the day, given this goal you will be constrained by how many variables you can discuss, which is not the case for the single holistic design, and is in fact one of its key strengths (see Section 3.2.4).

4.7.5   Weakness #2: Need to Control Context

Conducting a multiple case study with replication logic is similar to an experiment. The origins of this approach go back to John Stuart Mill's (1875) method of difference, where researchers set out to establish the effect of a specific factor. To establish this effect plausibly, other factors must be controlled for (to ensure that they are similar), so that the difference in outcome can be ascribed to a corresponding difference in the selected causes of interest (Gerring, 2007; King et al., 1994; Lijphart, 1975; Mahoney & Goertz, 2006):

> If an instance in which the phenomenon under investigation occurs, and an instance in which it does not occur have every circumstance in common, save one, then that one occurring only in the former, the circumstance in which alone the two instances differ is the effect, or the cause, or an indispensable part of the cause, of the phenomenon. (Mill, 1875: p. 452, cited in Blatter & Haverland, 2012: pp. 42–43)

The characteristics of the selected cases directly determine the possibility of the case researcher to make internally valid conclusions. Thus, a rigorous case study design is expected to not only stipulate explicitly the focal variables of theoretical interest (i.e. your independent and dependent variables), but also check for plausible alternative explanations. The cases should therefore exhibit strong differences with respect to the main independent variables and corresponding (theoretically motivated) differences on the dependent variable and otherwise be as similar as possible on other variables (i.e. control variables). This is where the difficulty comes in. Finding multiple cases whose certain characteristics allow us to explain a causal argument and whose other characteristics remain constant, or "controlled," is practically very difficult to achieve. As John Stuart Mill pointed out, "we can artificially create a suitable (case) or find one in nature which matches our expectations" (Mill, 1875). But, by definition, case study research does not allow for artificial manipulation. Hence, our job here is to find the right cases (i.e. those that exhibit the characteristics necessary to make causal claims). However, finding these right cases that can control for unwanted variables (i.e. by being similar on these variables) whilst simultaneously letting the dependent and independent variables vary is in fact quite challenging.

4.7.6   Weakness #3: Small Number of Independent Variables

The number of independent (causal or explanatory) variables that can be manipulated in an experimental design is necessarily small, since every additional variable exponentially increases the complexity of the research design by increasing the number of experimental cells for comparison (explained in Section 4.6). Similarly, case studies can also logically only investigate a determinate number of independent variables, since every additional variable exponentially increases the complexity of the design and the number of theoretically relevant cases. Apart from this technical issue, there is the practical challenge of finding cases that are sufficiently similar with regard to relevant variables that might provide alternative explanations to the focal variables. The more independent variables we have, the more explanatory variables need to be included for control, and the more difficult it gets to find cases that are similar on all these dimensions (Blatter & Haverland, 2012). In this sense, the analogy between case studies and experimental methods is more intuitive than between case studies and surveys, where the lack of experimental control allows for a much larger number of explanatory variables to be investigated. Confusingly, one of the most-often cited definitions of case studies is that of Yin (2013), who points out that case studies are appropriate when "there are more variables of interest than data points" (Yin, 2013: pp. 13–14). However, case studies do not easily handle large amounts of independent variables since that would make theory building from case studies overly complex and not plausible or "persuasive" in terms of internal validity (Siggelkow, 2007). It may also lead to findings which are simply idiosyncratic to the chosen case (which is an external validity problem).

4.8   Brief Summary

Multiple holistic case study designs have many strengths, despite their alleged weaknesses. We summarize the main strengths as follows and add to our Case Checklist in Table 4.1.

- The first strength is its capacity to undertake LR. As seen in Chapter 3 for the single holistic design, replication is not possible due to the

Table 4.1 *Checklist table on the strengths and weaknesses of case study designs*

	Type of Case Study Design	Strengths	Weaknesses
Archetypical case study designs	**Single Holistic**	□ Fine grained explanatory power (explain a process) □ Falsification □ Data access and construct validity □ Unlimited variables	□ Internal validity (can't undertake variance analysis) □ External validity (can't generalize findings to a population of cases)
	Multiple Holistic	□ Undertake literal replication (enhances reliability) □ Undertake theoretical replication (enhances internal validity) □ Undertake theoretical replication (enhances external validity)	□ Depth of observation is compromised □ Difficult to control for context (given that we cannot manipulate) □ Additional independent variable exponentially increases the complexity of research design
	Single Embedded	Soon to come in Chapter 5	Soon to come in Chapter 5
	Multiple Embedded	Soon to come in Chapter 6	Soon to come in Chapter 6

design limitation of the single holistic design (i.e. we literally have only one case here). Consequently, the fact that LR can be executed with the multiple holistic design (by virtue of it having more than one case), means we can also ensure reliability, as we will end up with similar cases that yield identical insights.

• The second strength is its capacity to undertake TR, which also enhances internal validity. This is because we can isolate by keeping control variables constant across the cases and by comparing the differences on the independent and dependent variables. Consequently, TR helps us to identify which independent variable brought about the effect or change on the dependent variable.

• The third strength is that, by virtue of undertaking TR, we are also accounting for a more representative set of cases. This is because, in TR, cases on either end of the extremes are selected. Therefore, by choosing TR in multiple holistic design, a researcher can enhance external validity.

Despite the strengths of this design, there are a number of weaknesses as well.

- The first being that the depth of observations is compromised when using a multiple holistic design. This constraint is eminent from the fact that we are dealing with more than one case. The higher the number of cases, the more the depth of observations will be compromised.
- The second weakness is the difficulty in controlling context for the comparative analysis between the cases.
- The third weakness is that the number of independent variables that can be manipulated in a multiple holistic design is small. This is because as you add more independent variables, the complexity of the research design increases exponentially.

REFERENCES

Acemoglu, D., & Robinson, J. A. (2012). *Why Nations Fail: The Origins of Power, Prosperity, and Poverty*. New York: Currency.

Anthony, A. (2018, September 29). So is it nature not nurture after all? *The Guardian*. Available at: www.theguardian.com/science/2018/sep/29/so-is-it-nature-not-nurture-after-all-genetics-robert-plomin-polygenic-testing (last accessed July 14, 2022).

Blatter, J. & Haverland, M. (2012). *Designing Case Studies: Explanatory Approaches in Small-N Research*. Basingstoke: Palgrave Macmillan.

Brody, J. (2018, August 20). What twins can teach us about nature vs. nurture. *The New York Times*. Available at: www.nytimes.com/2018/08/20/well/family/what-twins-can-teach-us-about-nature-vs-nurture.html (last accessed July 14, 2022).

Calder, B. J., Phillips, L. W. & Tybout, A. M. (1982). The concept of external validity. *Journal of Consumer Research*, 9(3), 240–244.

Cook, T. D. & Campbell, D. T. (1979). *Quasi-Experimentation: Design and Analysis for Field Settings*. Chicago: Rand McNally.

Dyer, W. G. & Wilkins, A. L. (1991). Better stories, not better constructs, to generate better theory: A rejoinder to Eisenhardt. *Academy of Management Review*, 6(3), 613–619.

Eisenhardt, K. M. (1989). Building theories from case study research. *Academy of Management Review*, 14(4), 532–550.

  (1991). Better stories and better constructs: The case for rigor and comparative logic. *Academy of Management Review*, 16(3), 620–627.

Eisenhardt, K. M. & Graebner, M. E. (2007). Theory building from cases: Opportunities and challenges. *Academy of Management Journal*, 50(1), 25–32.

Ericksen, E. P. (1988). A review: Estimating the concentration of wealth in America. *The Public Opinion Quarterly*, 52(2), 243–253.

Gehman, J., Glaser, V. L., Eisenhardt, K. M., Gioia, D., Langley, A. & Corley, K. G. (2017). Finding theory–method fit: A comparison of three qualitative approaches to theory building. *Journal of Management Inquiry*, 27(3), 284–300.

Gerring, J. (2007). *Case Study Research: Principles and Practices*. Cambridge: Cambridge University Press.

Gibbert, M. & Ruigrok, W. (2010). The "what" and "how" of case study rigor: Three strategies based on published work. *Organizational Research Methods*, 3(4), 710–737.

Gibbert, M., Ruigrok, W. & Wicki, B. (2008). What passes as a rigorous case study? *Strategic Management Journal*, 29(13), 1465–1474.

Glaser, B. & Strauss, A. (1967). *The Discovery of Grounded Theory*. Chicago: Aldine Press.

Grant, R. M. (2003). Strategic planning in a turbulent environment: Evidence from the oil majors. *Strategic Management Journal*, 24(6), 491–517.

James, O. (2016, February 27). How to raise a brilliant child without screwing them up. *The Guardian*. Available at: www.theguardian.com/lifeandstyle/2016/feb/27/how-to-raise-a-brilliant-child-without-screwing-them-up (last accessed July 14, 2022).

King, G., Keohane, R. O. & Verba, S. (1994). *Designing Social Inquiry*. Princeton: Princeton University Press.

Langley, A. (1999). Strategies for theorizing from process data. *Academy of Management Review*, 24(4), 691–710.

Lee, A. S. & Baskerville, R. L. (2003). Generalizing generalizability in information systems research. *Information Systems Research*, 14(3), 221–243.

Lijphart, A. (1975). The comparable-cases strategy in comparative research. *Comparative Political Studies*, 8(2), 158–177.

Lincoln, Y. & Guba, E. (1985). *Naturalistic Inquiry*. Beverly Hills: Sage.

Mahoney, J. & Goertz, G. (2006). A tale of two cultures: Contrasting quantitative and qualitative research. *Political Analysis*, 14(3), 227–249.

March, J. G., Sproull, L. S. & Tamuz, M. (1991). Learning from samples of one or fewer. *Organization Science*, 2(1), 1–13.

McGrath, J. E. & Brinberg, D. (1983). External validity and the research process: A comment on the Calder/Lynch dialogue. *Journal of Consumer Research*, 10 (1), 115–124.

Mill, J. S. (1875). *A System of Logic, Ratiocinative and Inductive: Being a Connected View of the Principles of Evidence and the Methods of Scientific Investigation*. London: Longmans, Green, Reader and Dyer.

Popper, K. (1959). *The Logic of Scientific Discovery*. Abingdon-on-Thames: Routledge.

Pratt, M. G., Kaplan, S. & Whittington, R. (2020). Editorial essay: The tumult over transparency: Decoupling transparency from replication in establishing trustworthy qualitative research. *Administrative Science Quarterly*, 65(1), 1–19.

Russell, B. (1912). *The Problems of Philosophy*. Oxford: Oxford University Press.

Schmidt, F. L. & Hunter, J. E. (1996). Measurement error in psychological research: Lessons from 26 research scenarios. *Psychological Methods*, 1(2), 199–223.

Schweizer, L. (2005). Organizational integration of acquired biotechnology companies into pharmaceutical companies: The need for a hybrid approach. *Academy of Management Journal*, 48(6), 1051–1074.

Siggelkow, N. (2007). Persuasion with case studies. *Academy of Management Journal*, 50(1), 20–24.

Stake, R. E. (1995). *The Art of Case Study Research*. Thousand Oaks: Sage.

Tsang, E. W., & Williams, J. N. (2012). Generalization and induction: Misconceptions, clarifications, and a classification of induction. *MIS Quarterly*, 36(3), 729–748.

Tsoukas, H. (2017). Don't simplify, complexify: From disjunctive to conjunctive theorizing in organization and management studies. *Journal of Management Studies*, 54(2), 132–153.

Welch, C., Piekkari, R., Plakoyiannaki, E., & Paavilainen-Mäntymäki, E. (2011). Theorising from case studies: Towards a pluralist future for international business research. *Journal of International Business Studies*, 42(5), 740–762.

Yin, R. K. (1981). The case study crisis: Some answers. *Administrative Science Quarterly*, 26(1), 58–65.

(2003). Designing case studies. *Qualitative Research Methods*, 5(14), 359–386.

(2013). *Case Study Research: Design and Methods*. Thousand Oaks: Sage.

CHAPTER 5

The Natural Experiment, a.k.a. the Single Embedded Design

5.1 Single Embedded Case Study Design: What Is It? Why Do We Need This Design?

Single embedded designs feature one case (that's why they are called "single") with at least two sub-units of analysis within that one case (these are the "embedded" units). It is a powerful design as it combines many of the strengths of the single case with basically all the strengths of the multiple design (in theoretical replication mode). And there's more: Because two sub-units of one overall case are compared, we "naturally" control for a lot of contextual variables (precisely by keeping the case context constant across the two sub-units). This is called "controlled comparison." Some people (including the Nobel Prize Commission) prefer to call them Natural Experiments, and like them so much that they awarded the 2021 Nobel Prize in Economics to David Card, Joshua D. Agrist, and Guido W. Imbens for their work in natural experiments, which afforded important methodological contributions to the analysis of causal relationships. Now, isn't that a good reason to take a closer look at this important design?

In their 2013 article, Slater and Ziblatt discussed the role of controlled comparison in politics using the example of government performance in Italy (Putnam, 1993). Instead of examining government performance in Italy as a single case (which would have been a single holistic design), Putnam explained the variation in government performance across the two broad geographical areas of northern and southern Italy through a single embedded case study. The within-case embedded units allowed Putnam to compare the comparative politics (no pun intended) in a single country. The areas were closely matched to each other and were naturally controlled for a wide array of national-level variables (e.g. Catholicism, parliamentarism, fascist legacies) which could have provided alternate explanations. Furthermore, the embedded units were also different in terms of their dependent variable (or outcome). Northern Italy was well governed as any other country in the OECD, whereas southern Italy was amongst the worst (Slater & Ziblatt, 2013). Thus, between the two embedded units (i.e. North and South) present within the single case (i.e. Italy), the full range of variation in industrialized democracies was displayed, even though only one case was studied. Through this study, Putnam (1993) revealed the role of social capital and civic engagement on government performance.

BUT BEFORE WE MOVE ON, LET'S THINK ABOUT ...

... THE KIND OF REPLICATION THAT PUTNAM (1993) UNDERTOOK WHEN SELECTING
THE TWO PROVINCES WITHIN ITALY
What are the control, independent and dependent variables in Putnam's study? Think about it before reading the discussion here.

Putnam's (1993) study is an example of single embedded design using theoretical replication. By controlling for national-level variables and selecting embedded units which are from both extremes of the theoretical prediction (Yin, 2013), Putnam made a clear claim about the role of social capital and civic engagement (independent variables) in government performance (dependent variable). Even more interestingly, Putnam allowed for the efficient assessment of the given study's representativeness by transparently discussing the rationale behind the case selection. As Eisenhardt points out, "in theory building from cases, the researcher is trying to, on one hand, control the extraneous variation, and on the other hand, focus attention on the variation of interest" (Gehman et al., 2018: p. 5). The logic Putnam and Eisenhardt suggest is to see how a change in the independent variable explains the variance on the dependent variable (Blatter & Haverland, 2012; Mohr, 1982). Italy was chosen as the case because it offered a great opportunity for research on the functioning of democracy and it was Putnam's country of expertise (Fabbrini, 2011; Putnam, 1993). The geographical areas were selected because of the vast variations in their outcome and the natural controls they offered (Slater & Ziblatt, 2013). See the strength of the single-embedded design here, compared to the multiple holistic design? Using the latter design and comparing two different countries in the OECD (say, Italy and Japan) would not have provided these natural controls or the consequential internal validity, which are the key strengths of embedded designs. You will recall that we needed an excuse to jump from single holistic designs to multiple designs. That excuse was to introduce theoretical replication and the pivotal role of comparing units of analysis (either single holistic cases in Chapter 4 or sub-units embedded in one case in the present chapter).

BUT BEFORE WE MOVE ON, LET'S THINK ABOUT . . .

. . . WHAT THE DIFFERENCE IS BETWEEN PUTNAM'S (1993) CHOICE OF CASE STUDY
DESIGN AND A MULTIPLE HOLISTIC DESIGN

Don't be afraid to be *imaginatively curious* and be enchanted by what is to follow.

5.2   What Makes the Single Embedded Design Different from the Multiple and Single Holistic Case Study Designs?

In this section, we discuss important distinctions of the single embedded case study design from the single holistic (discussed in Chapter 3) and multiple holistic (discussed in Chapter 4) case study designs.

5.2.1   Difference #1: Level of Analysis

The level of analysis indicates the level on which theory building is happening. The levels of analysis for the single holistic and multiple holistic designs take place at the level of the case, while for the single embedded case study design it happens not only at the case level but also within the case (i.e. with regards to the embedded units). Is this a little confusing? Let us explain this via our Putnam (1993) example. Here we want you to think about what Putnam's (1993) main object of concern is. More specifically which units are of theoretical interest to him? Well, for one, it is Italy (the case) which is his first level of analysis. If Putnam (1993) would stay at this level it would be a single holistic case study design. But as we know this is not what he did. Putnam went one level further down by zeroing in on the northern and southern provinces of Italy. Are the northern and southern provinces Putnam's objects of concern? Given that he is theoretically interested in them, we would say yes! It is because of this that the provinces represent another level of analysis.

BUT BEFORE WE MOVE ON, LET'S THINK ABOUT . . .

. . . WHAT PUTNAM WOULD HAVE NEEDED TO DO IF HE WANTED TO HAVE A
MULTIPLE HOLISTIC DESIGN

What do you think?

This means that, due to the presence of embedded units in the single embedded case study design, theory building now also happens within the case (which is not the case in either single or multiple holistic case study designs). Nota bene, however, that the main level of analysis remains the case level. Putnam uses the North/South divide to, let's say "artificially" generate two versions of the same country. That's almost like magic, isn't it? Effectively, Putnam clones Italy (well, at least he clones those variables that he does not want to influence the outcomes, the so-called control variables, such as Catholicism, parliamentarism, and fascist legacies). At the same time, the range of variance between the two sub-units in terms of the explanatory variables, that is, the social capital and civic engagement, as well as the dependent variable, that is, the government performance, approximates the range of variance of the least and most developed countries in the OECD and is therefore even generalizable to the population. Can you see how the main level of analysis remains on the case level? Putnam is not interested in the North and the South per se, but uses them as a means to an end, and that end is to make inferences about other countries (not geographical areas of other countries) in the OECD. It just so happens, "naturally" that Italy provides the unique opportunity to compare two countries in a highly controlled context of only one country. If this sounds complicated, turn it around: If indeed, the main level of analysis were on the sub-units, rather than on the case, the case would disappear, right? If we compare units of analysis without a case holding them together in some way, we are looking at a multiple design!

5.2.2 Difference #2: Replication

The second important distinction between the single embedded and single and multiple holistic design is the presence and the nature of replication. As indicated in the earlier chapter, replication is when a researcher chooses more than one dissimilar and/or similar cases (Yin, 2013) to compare findings of the initial cases with. In this regard, replication is useful as it allows researchers to undertake cross-case comparisons (Eisenhardt, 1989; Yin, 2013). While the term "replication" has been reserved for multiple case study design (Eisenhardt, 1989; Eisenhardt & Graebner, 2007; Yin, 2013) so far, it can also be extended for the single embedded case study design (Hoorani et al., 2019). That is, a single embedded case study design can replicate findings from the analysis on embedded units by comparing it with other, dissimilar (and/or similar) embedded units, in a process known as theoretical replication. Such comparisons between embedded units establish the effect of the independent variable on the dependent variable. As already explained in Chapter 4, theoretical replication is akin to John Stuart Mill's (1875) method of difference. The aim, as discussed in Chapter 4, is to isolate the effect of an independent variable on the dependent variable while holding control variables constant.

Therefore, while replication is possible for the single embedded design, it is not possible for the single holistic design (Hoorani et al., 2019) as there is literally just one case (or unit of analysis). Now you may ask – what about the multiple holistic case study design? Isn't replication happening in that design? So, what is the difference here? Well, yes. You are right, but the nature of replication in a multiple holistic design differs from that of a single embedded design. Coming back to our old friend Putnam (1993), he is replicating within the case by selecting two provinces within Italy. We call this "within-case comparison." The provinces, as indicated, are on a different level of analysis. If Putnam (1993) was interested in a multiple holistic design then he should have undertaken a cross-country comparison by selecting different countries (e.g. Switzerland, France, Germany), also known as "between-cases comparison" (more to come on within-case and between-cases comparison in Chapter 6).

BUT BEFORE WE MOVE ON, LET'S THINK ABOUT …

… THE KIND OF DESIGN YOU WOULD GENERATE IF REPLICATION WERE TO HAPPEN WITHIN-CASE AS WELL AS AT THE CASE LEVEL

Be imaginatively curious about it BUT, if you want to learn right away, then read Chapter 6.

5.3   Selection Rationale and Sampling for the Case(s)

In this section and in this chapter, we dive more deeply into explaining how selection can be done for the case(s). In earlier chapters, more specifically in Chapter 4, we already introduced theoretical sampling and how "theoretical" or "literal" replication can be used to select cases. In this section, we further expand on that explanation by highlighting other possible ways through which a case can be selected. In short, while the selection strategies discussed in this section are relevant to the single embedded case study design, they are also relevant for other case study designs (i.e. single holistic, multiple holistic, multiple embedded).

It is important here to highlight, first and foremost, that the selection or qualitative sampling differs considerably from quantitative sampling on three fronts. First, while the primary aim of quantitative sampling is to select a sample that is representative of the population; the aim of qualitative sampling is to select few but informationally rich cases that can provide maximum insights into the phenomenon under investigation (Patton, 2002; Yin, 2013). The reason for the latter way of selection is that the "typical" or the "average case" is not always the most informative (Flyvbjerg, 2006). Hence, in qualitative studies statistical generalizability of the results is not the key goal (Stake, 1995; Yin, 2013). Second, in case study research, selecting a case and analyzing it are two very intertwined processes (Gerring & Seawright, 2006). This means that, unlike quantitative sampling, which is conducted in the initial stages of research, qualitative sampling can be an ongoing process. Hence, in this regard, the selection of qualitative case(s) is quite flexible, that is, in light of new insights derived from the analysis of initial cases(s) the researchers can decide to select more cases or embedded units. More on this in Chapters 7 and 8, where we introduce the sequencing of case study designs. Third, in quantitative sampling, there is little variation when it comes to different sampling techniques; however, this is not true for qualitative sampling (Elman et al., 2016). For example, in political science, Seawright and Gerring (2008) have suggested nine different case selection techniques, which are *typical, diverse, extreme, deviant, influential, crucial, pathway, most-similar,* and *most-different*. In international business, Welch et al. (2016) also suggested four strategies for selecting cases, most likely case sampling, least likely case sampling, sub-group sampling, and paired comparison with the aim of concept reconstruction. More recently, Fletcher et al. (2018) have suggested two types of sampling strategies for case study research: Theory- and phenomenon-driven case selection strategies. While a theory-driven selection strategy resorts to an existing theory for selecting the case, the latter strategy draws on the phenomenon itself.

Another more well accepted case selection technique is theoretical sampling, also discussed in Chapter 4, in which a theory acts as a guiding compass to select a case(s) (Eisenhardt, 1989; Glaser & Strauss, 1967; Strauss & Corbin, 1998). Replication can be applied for conducting theoretical sampling if there is more than one case to select. However, theoretical sampling also works if there is only one case that needs to be selected. For example, in management, Vuori and Huy (2016) selected

Nokia as their case. Their interest was to understand Nokia's failure in producing a smartphone after Apple had introduced the iPhone. They justify the selection of the case by discussing how it allowed them to "develop a deeper understanding of the emergence of shared emotions during the innovation process and (how they) influence innovation because it represents an extreme case for theory building" (Vuori & Huy, 2016: p. 11). Another well-known selection technique is convenience sampling, in which the cases that are most easily accessible are selected (Etikan et al., 2016; Patton, 2002). For example, the geographical proximity of the case or easy/good access to data sources could motivate convenience sampling.

Our intention is not to overwhelm you with the multiple ways in which a case(s) can be selected. However, what this methodological proliferation of case selection strategies highlights is the centrality of case selection to case study research. This is because the inferential power of case study design rests quite literally upon the case(s) that the researcher selects, since different cases may lead to different insights (Ragin, 1992; Rihoux & Ragin, 2008). As Geddes (1990) aptly reminds us "the cases we choose determine the answers we get" (p. 131). Hence, without a clear understanding of how a researcher selects the case(s), one is hard-pressed to determine the reliability and suitability of conclusions reached, thus inducing direct consequences on the rigor of a case study (Cuervo-Cazurra et al., 2016; Eisenhardt & Graebner, 2007; Gerring & Cojocaru, 2016; Patton, 2002).

Nonetheless, in spite of the many case selection strategies, we see all these techniques falling under the umbrella of *purposeful sampling*. That is the intent of all these diverse selection strategies – to help in selecting the most "information rich" case(s) that "purposefully fit" the aim of the study (Patton, 2002). More importantly, we want to stress that the selection of case(s) in qualitative case study research is not a singular or static decision. Therefore, selection strategies in case studies can be used individually or together with other strategies. For instance, this combination of selection strategies often happens in case studies following a theoretical sampling technique. Since theoretical sampling is often guided by emerging theory from prior data collection and analysis episodes, it is usually used only after the first round of data collection and analysis is completed. Hence, it often succeeds another sampling strategy, but more to come on that in Chapter 7.

5.4 Longitudinal and/or Cross-sectional Single Embedded Designs

BUT BEFORE WE MOVE ON, LET'S THINK ABOUT …

… LONGITUDINAL AND CROSS-SECTIONAL DESIGNS FOR THE SINGLE HOLISTIC AND
MULTIPLE HOLISTIC CASE STUDY

Fill out Table 5.1.

Table 5.1 *Longitudinal and/or cross-sectional single embedded designs exercise*

Scenario#	Single holistic longitudinal case study design	Single holistic cross-sectional case study design	Multiple holistic longitudinal case study design	Multiple holistic cross-sectional case study design
	Be imaginatively curious and think of your own examples			

Create your own hypothetical scenarios by being imaginatively curious!
Scenario #1:
Scenario #2:
Scenario #3:
Scenario #4:
After filling out the table of this box insert think about the following
questions:

Q.1 Can you provide an example on how a combined longitudinal and
cross-sectional study will look in a single holistic design? Explain
and justify.

Q.2 Can you provide an example on how a combined longitudinal and
cross-sectional study will look in a multiple holistic design? Explain
and justify.

Anyway, coming back to our single embedded case study design, unlike
the single holistic design (but like the multiple holistic), it is able to offer
different design possibilities, because of the involved replication. Regarding
the nature of embedded units (or sub-cases) they can be either spatial

(i.e. synchronic or cross-sectional) or temporal (i.e. diachronic or longitudinal) in nature (Gerring, 2004; Miles & Huberman, 1994; Yin, 2013). Spatial embedded units (such as the North and South of Italy in Putnam's case) can be seen as units of analysis that lack a temporal dimension and, hence, is cross-sectional in nature. On the other hand, temporal embedded units are units of analysis (your objects of interest) that have a temporal dimension. Such a design helps to control for the spatial context substantially as it is the same case being observed at different points in time.

Therefore, replication can be done using spatial embedded units and/or temporal embedded units within the case. Depending on which type of embedded unit is selected, the researcher can design a cross-sectional or a longitudinal single embedded case study. A combination of cross-sectional and longitudinal designs together in a single embedded case study is also a possibility. This, therefore, makes the single embedded design richer from a design perspective when compared to a single holistic design, since the latter by virtue of the single case is void of any possible comparative analysis.

5.4.1   Cross-sectional Design

A cross-sectional study using the single embedded case study design will comprise of spatial embedded units within the case for a given point in time. Given that there are spatial embedded units within the case, the researchers can undertake cross-sectional comparisons in which the temporal context can be controlled for. They can also simultaneously control for spatial context in the case since these spatial embedded units are present within the same case.

For example, in the field of political science, Collier and Collier (2002) selected Latin America and then went on to look at certain countries within the region (i.e. Brazil, Chile, Mexico, Venezuela, Uruguay, Columbia, Argentina, and Peru). Such a comparative historical analysis of eight countries within Latin America allowed Collier and Collier (2002) to theorize about a period in which major political reorientation was happening, thus providing important insights into changes from a repressive state to a state embracing labor movements. So, what is the case, and what are the spatial embedded units in the above-mentioned example? We are quite sure that you have gotten this right – Latin America is the case, and the countries are the spatial embedded units. In International Business, Gutierrez-Huerter et al. (2020) looked at an organization and its foreign subsidiaries. Their focus was to understand translation of corporate social responsibility reporting from the MNE headquarters to its foreign subsidiaries. So, what is the case, and what are the spatial embedded units in this example? We are quite sure that you have gotten this right again – the organization is the case and the foreign subsidiaries are spatial embedded units. In the field of management research, De Toni and Pessot (2021) investigate a leading company in the shipbuilding industry, by analyzing seven projects within the organization to unpack the relationship between project complexity and organizational learning. They see the seven projects as "representative of the overall project management process" (De Toni & Pessot, 2021: p. 545). Moreover, the seven projects provide the right variance on "product (in terms of size and technological newness), product development process (referring to the shipyard, i.e. the production site, as well as the stage of development corresponding to the phase within the project life cycle), and project management issues" (p. 545). Here we stop short from asking you what the case and the spatial embedded units are in this scenario. Instead, we are more curious to know if you have picked up on something peculiar about these examples.

BUT BEFORE WE MOVE ON, LET'S THINK ABOUT …

... THE THREE MULTIDISCIPLINARY EXAMPLES DISCUSSED

But first let us also read the following example from the field of psychology.

Blue Eyes/Brown Eyes Experiment

Imagine you are a third-grade teacher and recently Martin Luther King Junior has been assassinated. You think it is important for you to explain to your third graders the adverse consequences of racism and discrimination on individuals, groups of people, and communities. You discuss this with your third graders, but you realize that your third graders are not fully grasping the deep impact of racism and discrimination; and you decide that they really need to experience it for themselves to empathize with this issue. What do you do? Well you divide your third graders into two groups, one group includes only blue-eyed children and the other group consists of brown eyed children. Then, you as the teacher actively discriminate these two groups on the first day of the class by giving preferential treatment to one group, and not to the other. And on the second day, you reverse your preferential treatment to the other group. You see that children belonging to the "preferential treatment" group were performing better when compared to children belonging to the "non-preferential" group. Are we telling you a fictional story? Well, no, as this activity was actually conducted by Mrs. Elliott in 1968 on her third graders (also read the *New York Times* article by Gupta (2020)). This social experiment allowed her third graders to understand the nature and consequences of racism and discrimination better. Coming back to the case study designs, this could be seen as a single embedded design. We now let you decide what is the case and what are the embedded units here!

Now, for this thinking exercise, fill out Table 5.2 and think about the question posed after that.

Table 5.2 *Thinking exercise*

	Exercise			
	Example #1 (Collier & Collier, 2002)	Example #2	Example #3	Example #4
Disciplines	**Political Science**	**International Business**	**Management**	**Psychology**
What is the case?	Latin America Region	Organization		
What are the spatial embedded units?	Countries	Foreign subsidiaries		
Let's be imaginatively curious! **What other kind of single cases can possibly be selected from each discipline?**				
What other kind of spatial embedded units can possibly be selected from each discipline?				

Q. Coming back to the *Blue Eyes/Brown Eyes Experiment*, what kind of replication is taking place within-case here? (*Hint*: think in terms of what we learnt in Chapter 4 on literal and theoretical replication.)

So, did you catch something peculiar in the examples that we discussed? In fact, how about you look at your filled out "Exercise table'" in the previous box insert. What is visibly noticeable here is that the boundaries of the case and the nature of spatially embedded units can vary considerably. Frankly there is no real limit to how big or small a case(s) and/or embedded units can be. For example, depending upon the purpose and research questions of the concerned studies, it can range from countries to cities to industries to organizations to departments to societies to communities to groups and even to individuals (Fletcher & Plakoyiannaki, 2011). Moreover, the disciplinary leaning of the researchers might also inform the nature of the cases and embedded units. For example, in political science or international business, selecting a country as a case and different regions within the country as embedded units might be considered as mainstream (e.g. Putnam's study). But this may not be mainstream for a psychologist or a management scholar. Nonetheless we don't want to propose a rule of thumb here regarding what you can select or not select. At the end it all boils down to your "black hole," that is, your research question! Anyways, enough about cross-sectional designs; now let's discuss longitudinal designs for the single embedded case study.

BUT BEFORE WE MOVE ON, LET'S THINK ABOUT …

… HOW A CROSS-SECTIONAL STUDY WOULD LOOK FOR A MULTIPLE
HOLISTIC DESIGN

Think of new examples or, if you want, you can refer to the examples indicated in Chapter 4.

Q.1 Once you have revisited and formulated a cross-sectional multiple holistic design, can you see how this differs from the single embedded cross-sectional case study design? (*Hint*: You can always refer to Section 5.2 for inspiring your imaginative curiosity.)

Q.2 Can you think of an example of a cross-sectional single holistic case study design?

5.4.2 Longitudinal Design

A study using the longitudinal single embedded case study design comprises only temporal embedded units. Therefore, one of the key strengths of this design is that it can leverage the longitudinal (or temporal) dimension of the phenomenon to build theoretical insights by comparing selected temporal embedded units. An advantage of such a comparison is that it allows for variance-based theorizing (Blatter & Haverland, 2012) by ensuring contextual homogeneity so that factors that are affecting the phenomenon can be isolated (Yin, 2013) (already highlighted in Section 5.4). But more fundamental here is to understand the nature of temporal embedded units. Apart from being a researcher's object of interest, the temporal embedded unit also encompasses both the independent (cause) and dependent (outcome) variables.

A classic political science example where a longitudinal design was used for a single case study with temporal embedded units is the case study of Middletown (Lynd & Lynd, 1929, 1937). In their seminal work, the Lynds systematically compared the same medium sized American city along a variety of dependent variables before the Great depression (Lynd & Lynd, 1929) and after the Great depression (Lynd & Lynd, 1937). Studying the same city along the same variables at two different time periods allowed them to control contextual factors (that were of no interest to the study in hand), and as a result allowed them to identify changes in the social structure with the start of the Great depression. In analogy to experimental studies, the temporal comparison in the Middletown case study can be termed "theoretical replication" (Eisenhardt, 1989; Yin, 2013), where the researcher selected two (or more) temporal units for studying them along the same dependent and independent variables. However, this examination is now taking place within the case. Another example in the field of political science is Skocpol's (1979) work on identifying independent (causal) variables that trigger a social revolution. For the French revolution, she identified three stages of a social revolution, which are "the collapse of the old regime," "mass mobilization of the peasantry class," and the "reconsolidation of power by a new elite." One can draw parallels of this analysis to a longitudinal single embedded design, where the French Revolution is the case and the three stages/periods are the temporally embedded units.

Similarly, the experiment conducted by psychologist Mary Cover Jones to remove Peter's fear of rabbits (Jones, 1924) can also be seen as an example of single embedded case study design. Here Peter (being the case) would start crying whenever he was introduced to a rabbit. To remove his fear of rabbits, he was introduced to a rabbit over multiple periods of time (temporal embedded units). It started off by Peter being introduced to the rabbit at a distance (12 feet away). But every time the rabbit was brought closer to Peter, he was given a candy. At some point, Peter was able to touch the rabbit without crying. By pairing the rabbit (the fear stimuli) with the candy (pleasure stimuli), Peter was able to overcome his fear over time.

BUT BEFORE WE MOVE ON, LET'S THINK ABOUT ...

... THE ABOVE SINGLE EMBEDDED CASE STUDY DESIGN CONDUCTED BY MARY
COVER JONES ON PETER

The case is _____

Q.1 Can you indicate what the case is?
Q.2 Can you indicate what the controls are?
Q.3 For each temporal embedded unit (for simplicity purposes let's assume three) can you think of the possible independent and dependent variables?

BUT SOMEONE TOLD ME THAT ...

... LONGITUDINAL DESIGNS DO NOT NEED TEMPORAL EMBEDDED UNITS

Well that someone is indeed right. Having temporal embedded units in a longitudinal design is one of the many ways in which a researcher can engage with time. To explain this, we need to revisit Section 3.2.1, where we discuss "Process Studies and Jigsaws." Do you remember the process underlying Bob's bank robbery? Were there any temporal embedded units? The answer is no! And this is because there were no time periods identified that encapsulated both the independent and dependent variables that were being compared to one another, which is why it was a single holistic case study design. So, what was happening there? Well the process proposed in Chapter 3 was simply capturing the temporal flow that was void of any comparative analysis. To summarize, when unpacking a process in the single holistic design the interest is in the individual pieces (i.e. variables) and how they connect with each other to explain the temporal progression of the phenomenon.

BUT BEFORE WE MOVE ON, LET'S THINK ABOUT ...

... THE REASONING BEHIND SELECTING PETER AS THE CASE IN THE RABBIT-
FEAR STUDY

Read the following excerpt from Mary Cover Jones (1924) paper:

The case of Peter illustrates how a fear may be removed under laboratory conditions. His case was selected from a number of others for the following reasons:

(1) Progress in combating the fear reactions was so marked that many of the details of the process could be observed easily.

(2) It was possible to continue the study over a period of more than three months.

(3) The notes of a running diary show the characteristics of a healthy, normal, interesting child, well adjusted, except for his exaggerated fear reactions. (p. 308)

Q. In light of what was discussed in Section 5.3, can you indicate what strategies for case selection are being discussed by Mary Cover Jones?

Are you wondering how the jigsaw example fits with a single embedded case study design that has temporal embedded units? It is not that complicated, but before we can showcase it visually, we use a non-fictional example discussed by cultural criminologist Mike Presdee in his book "Cultural Criminology and the Carnival of Crime" (Presdee, 2003). Imagine that you land in the year 1992 via a time machine. You put your travel back in time to good use by asking yourself why large-scale joy riding (i.e. driving dangerously/criminally fast) is a persistent problem in neighborhood X in Oxford. You begin your investigation by conducting field observations. You notice that the neighborhood seems to have high unemployment (observation #1). You interview one of the shopkeepers (interviewee #1) and a police officer (interviewee #2), both of whom corroborate your observation. You understand now that there is unemployment, but why? By interviewing more local people (interviewees #3, 4, & 6) you learn that there was a car factory that recently closed. You realize that there are two time periods that need to be compared. The time when the car factory was open and the time when it got closed. You now actively compare both time periods on the variables (let's say, for simplicity's sake) – job opportunities and joyriding. You find that the car factory created job opportunities and no joyriding incidents, but when the car factory closed there was an absence of job opportunities and hence a presence of joyriding incidents. Now look at Figure 5.1, how do you think the jigsaw analogy fits here? Instead of focusing on the individual pieces (as in Chapter 3), here you are interested in comparing similarities and differences among puzzles (i.e. among temporal embedded units #1 and #2).

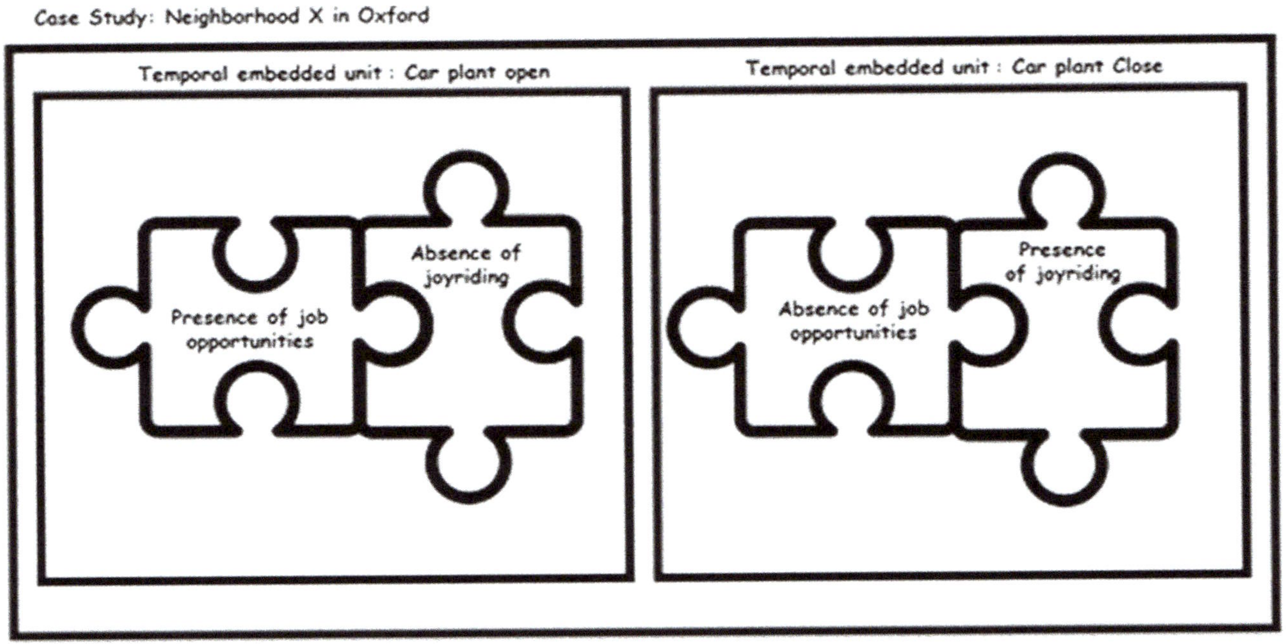

Figure 5.1 A jigsaw visual of longitudinal design for the single embedded case study

5.4.3   Cross-sectional and Longitudinal Designs

The single embedded case study design can select both spatial (cross-sectional) and temporal (longitudinal) embedded units to strengthen its comparative analysis. This offers a stronger design since both cross-sectional and longitudinal dimensions are being leveraged and compared. A famous historical example of a cross-sectional, longitudinal single embedded design is John Snow's natural experiment. The case was the city of London, and the spatially embedded units were two companies – the Lambeth Water Company and Southwark & Vauxhall Company, both of which provided water to the same neighborhoods. The only underlying difference between the two companies was their water source. The Lambeth water company had access to a fresher water site, since its intake pipe was located upstream of the Thames; while Southwark & Vauxhall company had access to a polluted site (also see Zielinski, 2010). Consequently, given that there were a higher number of deaths for households receiving water from Southward & Vauxhall Company than Lambeth Water Company, Snow was able to infer that the disease cholera was in fact waterborne. Here, a cross-sectional comparison was undertaken by comparing the two water companies (i.e. spatial embedded units), which were providing water to the same neighborhoods in London.

The temporally embedded units of this case study were the before (pre-1852) and after (post-1852) Lambeth Water Company. Pre-1852 Lambeth Water Company had the same water source as the Southwark & Vauxhall Company. However, in 1852 the Lambeth Water Company moved its water intake to a cleaner site. The post-Lambeth Water company was therefore another temporally embedded unit which was investigated. Here, the period before 1852 (i.e. first temporal embedded unit) when both companies had the same water source was compared with the period after 1852 (i.e. second temporal embedded unit), when both companies had different water sources (see Figure 5.2). While Snow's experiment has received criticism from the quantitative folks (e.g. see Koch & Denike, 2006), it is still relevant in terms of understanding the thought process behind devising a design in social settings where we as researchers cannot artificially impose controls.

Case study: London

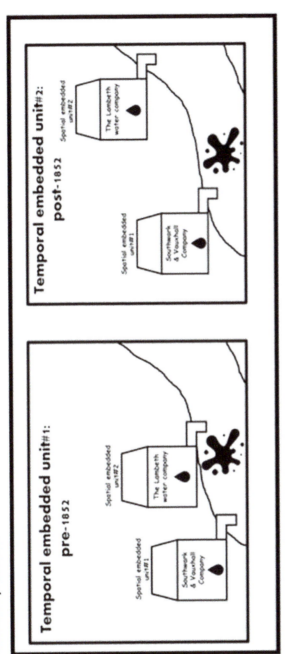

Figure 5.2 A visual representation of John Snow's single embedded case study design

95

BUT BEFORE WE MOVE ON, LET'S THINK ABOUT …

… THE KIND OF REPLICATION THAT IS TAKING PLACE IN JOHN SNOW'S EXPERIMENT
Look at Figure 5.2 again and think about the following questions.

Q.1   What kind of replication is taking place with respect to the two spatial
       embedded units in temporal embedded unit #1 (i.e. pre-1852)? (*Hint*:
       Think about the different types of replication discussed in Chapter 4.)
Q.2   What kind of replication is taking place for the two spatial embedded
       units in temporal embedded unit #2 (i.e. post-1852)? (*Hint*: Think
       about the different types of replication discussed in Chapter 4.)
Q.3   Coming back to the Garden of Eden example, can you design a single
       embedded case study by incorporating both spatial and temporal
       embedded units? Try to be creative and feel free to bring in Steve and
       Ava, apart from Adam and Eve.

AND/OR
By being imaginatively curious, create your own "Grand experiment"
(design #2). For both or either of the designs indicate the following:

(I)   What are your independent, dependent, and control variables?
(II)   What is your single case?
(III)   What are your spatial and temporal embedded units?
(IV)   What kind of replication is being undertaken?

In summary, there are several options for researchers interested in
conducting single embedded case studies. But what are the pros and cons
of undertaking single embedded case study research? We explain the
strengths and weaknesses of the design next.

5.5   Strengths and Weaknesses

5.5.1   Strength #1: Internal Validity

A single embedded case study design undertaking TR (Theoretical
Replication) is more internally valid than the single holistic design and
LR (Literal Replication) multiple holistic designs due to the simultaneous
presence of both replication logic and the "natural" controls. While the
natural controls ensure that the effects of specific independent variables are
correctly captured, the use of replication logic allows the researchers to pick
comparable embedded units. The embedded units exhibit all the variables
of interest (dependent and independent) and are otherwise as similar as

possible (control variables), precisely to make them comparable, that is, to allow the attribution of the variation to the independent variable(s). The focus of single embedded case studies is thus to understand the covariational differences between the independent variable and dependent variable for each individual (spatial and/or temporal) embedded units. Any causal relationship offered by the single embedded case study is thus a product of within-case comparison in the presence of natural controls.

5.5.2 Strength #2: External Validity (Stronger than the Single Holistic Case Study Design)

Another strength of single embedded designs is their external validity, as evidenced by Putnam's (1993) classic (cross-sectional) study of northern and southern Italy. These two embedded units captured the full range of variance in industrialized democracies, thus allowing for an efficient assessment of the study's representativeness or similarity with other unstudied cases in OECD. With diligent case selection as done by Putnam (1993), we can ensure that the embedded case study allows for generalization to a population beyond the single case.

Another classic (longitudinal) example is the case study of Middletown (Lynd & Lynd, 1929, 1937). In their seminal work, the Lynds systematically compared the same American medium sized city, which is the case, along a variety of dependent variables (i.e. six activities) before the Great depression (Lynd & Lynd, 1929), and after the Great depression (Lynd & Lynd, 1937). In this situation the period before and after the Great Depression can be seen as temporal embedded units selected via "theoretical replication" (Eisenhardt, 1989; Yin, 2013). Studying the same city along the same variables at two different time periods allowed them to control contextual factors (that were of no interest) and, as a result, allowed them to identify changes in social structure with the start of the Great depression. Since Middletown represented the average typical small American city, from an external validity perspective the selected single case allowed for generalizability to other small American cities that shared the same characteristics as Middletown.

5.5.3 Weakness #1: Small Number of Explanatory Variables

Unlike the single holistic case study that allows for the inclusion of many explanatory variables, the single embedded design, by virtue of its design that exploits comparative analysis, can only account for a small number of

Table 5.3 *Checklist table on the strengths and weakness of case study designs*

	Type of Case Study Design	Strengths	Weaknesses
Archetypical case study designs	**Single Holistic**	☐ Fine grained explanatory power (explain a process) ☐ Falsification ☐ Data access and construct validity ☐ Unlimited variables	☐ Internal validity (because can't undertake variance analysis) ☐ External validity (can't generalize findings to a population of cases)
	Multiple Holistic	☐ Undertake literal replication (enhances reliability) ☐ Undertake theoretical replication (enhances internal validity) ☐ Undertake theoretical replication (enhances external validity)	☐ Depth of observation is compromised ☐ Difficult to control for context (given that we cannot manipulate) ☐ Additional independent variable exponentially increases the complexity of the research design
	Single Embedded	☐ Higher internal validity (compared to single holistic and LR multiple holistic case study designs). ☐ TR single embedded design has a higher external validity (compared to the single holistic design, and to LR in a multiple holistic design).	☐ Smaller number of explanatory variables (when compared to the single holistic case study design). ☐ External validity of a TR single embedded design will be lower than a TR multiple case study design.
	Multiple Embedded	Soon to come in Chapter 6	Soon to come in Chapter 6

explanatory variables. It is also for this reason that the single holistic design can incorporate in-depth contextual insights (Dyer & Wilkins, 1991), whereas the single embedded design has to control for extraneous variations so as to identity independent variable(s) that produced the dependent variable(s). For example, in John Snow's experiment the independent variable was the source of water intake. Likewise, Skocpol (1979), in her effort to understand social revolutions, identified two independent variables that created a revolutionary scenario, that is, the presence of a "crisis state" and a "pattern of class dominance." According to Skocpol, the presence of these two independent variables would trigger a social revolution (i.e. the dependent variable). All in all, as evident from our examples, a single embedded design can account for only a small number of explanatory variables, at least when compared to the single holistic case study design.

5.5.4 Weakness #2: External Validity (Weaker than the Multiple Case Study Design)

External validity of the single embedded design is higher than that of the single holistic design, simply because it can account for more variation by undertaking theoretical replication within the case.

Although external validity of the single embedded case study designs is seen as higher compared to its holistic counterparts, it is however lower when compared to multiple case studies undertaking TR, precisely because these do not have "natural" controls and as such provide causal insight across more contextual variables. As we explained in Putnam's study, the single case (Italy) is chosen for the range of variance in independent and dependent variables in the two sub-units (North and South) which approximates the range of variance of the population (least and most developed countries in the OECD) and, therefore, affords the researcher to generalize to that population. Despite this, comparing two different countries with a similar range of variance (say, Japan and Botswana) affords greater generalizability precisely because they are so different when it comes to control variables. But this of course comes at the cost of internal validity, so why bother?

In fact, many qualitative researchers would see, as discussed in detail in Chapter 4, theoretical/analytical generalizability as more appropriate and would not see external validity as a relevant criterion here. If this is the case, then it is important to detail the contextual richness of the case. Providing these complex specificities and the context-specific findings of a well-conducted single embedded case study could thus lead to the refinement and reconsideration of social science concepts and theories. However, to do so, the researchers should explicitly account for and discuss the contextual issues, applied research procedures, and the concerned study's theoretical framework in their final reports.

5.6   Brief Summary

Single embedded case study designs include both strong and weak aspects. We summarize the key strengths along with weaknesses here and indicate them in our Case Checklist in Table 5.3.

- The first strength is that a single embedded case study design undertaking TR has higher internal validity when compared to the single holistic as well as multiple holistic case study designs undertaking LR. This is because, unlike the other two designs, the single embedded case study design undertaking TR can in tandem have both replication (inside the case) as well as ensure natural controls.
- The second strength is that it has a higher external validity than the single holistic design.
- The first weakness is that it has a smaller number of explanatory variables when compared to the single holistic case study design. Consequently, the single embedded design does not have the same design capacity to engage with the contextual richness of the case, when compared to the single holistic design that can provide deeper and richer contextualized explanations.
- The second weakness is that the external validity of a single embedded design will be lower than a multiple case study design.

REFERENCES

Blatter, J. & Haverland, M. (2012). *Designing Case Studies: Explanatory Approaches in Small-N Research.* London: Palgrave Macmillan.

Collier, R. B. & Collier, D. (2002). *Shaping the Political Arena: Critical Junctures, the Labor Movement, and Regime Dynamics in Latin America.* Notre Dame: University of Notre Dame Press.

Cuervo-Cazurra, A., Andersson, U., Brannen, M. Y., Nielsen, B. B. & Reuber, A. R. (2016). From the editors: Can I trust your findings? Ruling out alternative explanations in international business research. *Journal of International Business Studies*, 47(8), 881–897.

De Toni, A. F. & Pessot, E. (2021). Investigating organisational learning to master project complexity: An embedded case study. *Journal of Business Research*, 129, 541–554.

Dyer, W. G. & Wilkins, A. L. (1991). Better stories, not better constructs, to generate better theory: A rejoinder to Eisenhardt. *Academy of Management Review*, 6(3), 613–619.

Eisenhardt, K. M. (1989). Building theories from case study research. *Academy of Management Review*, 14(4), 532–550.

Eisenhardt, K. M. & Graebner, M. E. (2007). Theory building from cases: Opportunities and challenges. *Academy of Management Journal*, 50(1), 25–32.

Elman, C., Gerring, J. & Mahoney, J. (2016). Case study research: Putting the quant into the qual. *Sociological Methods Research*, 45(3), 375–391.

Etikan, I., Musa, S. A. & Alkassim, R. S. (2016). Comparison of convenience sampling and purposive sampling. *American Journal of Theoretical and Applied Statistics*, 5(1), 1–4.

Fabbrini, S. (2011). Robert D. Putnam between Italy and the United States. Bulletin of Italian *Politics*, 3(2), 391–399.

Fletcher, M. & Plakoyiannaki, E. (2011). Case selection in international business: key issues and common misconceptions. In R. Piekkari & C. Welch (eds.) *Rethinking the Case Study in International Business and Management Research*. Cheltenham: Edward Elgar Publishing, 171–191.

Fletcher, M., Zhao, Y., Plakoyiannaki, E. & Buck, T. (2018). Three pathways to case selection in international business: A twenty-year review. *Analysis and Synthesis. International Business Review*, 27(4), 755–766.

Flyvbjerg, B. (2006). Five misunderstandings about case-study research. *Qualitative Inquiry*, 12(2), 219–245.

Geddes, B. (1990). How the cases you choose affect the answers you get: Selection bias in comparative politics. *Political Analysis*, 2, 131–150.

Gehman, J., Glaser, V. L., Eisenhardt, K. M., Gioia, D., Langley, A. & Corley, K. G. (2018). Finding theory–method fit: A comparison of three qualitative approaches to theory building. *Journal of Management Inquiry*, 27(3), 284–300.

Gerring, J. (2004). What is a case study and what is it good for? *American Political Science Review*, 98(2), 341–354.

Gerring, J. & Cojocaru, L. (2016). Selecting cases for intensive analysis: A diversity of goals and methods. *Sociological Methods & Research*, 45(3), 392–423.

Gerring, J. & Seawright, J. (2006). Techniques for choosing cases. In J. Gerring (ed.) *Case Study Research: Principles and Practices*. Cambridge: Cambridge University Press, 86–150.

Glaser, B. & Strauss, A. (1967). *The Discovery of Grounded Theory*. Piscataway: Aldine Press.

Gupta, A. H. (2020, July 4). A teacher held a famous racism exercise in 1968. She's still at it. *New York Times*. Available at: www.nytimes.com/2020/07/04/us/jane-elliott-anti-racism-blue-eyes-brown-eyes.html (last accessed July 19, 2022).

Gutierrez-Huerter O, G., Moon, J., Gold, S. & Chapple, W. (2020). Micro-processes of translation in the transfer of practices from MNE headquarters to foreign subsidiaries: The role of subsidiary translators. *Journal of International Business Studies*, 51(3), 389–413.

Hoorani, B. H., Nair, L. B. & Gibbert, M. (2019). Designing for impact: The effect of rigor and case study design on citations of qualitative case studies in management. *Scientometrics*, 121(1), 285–306.

Jones, M. (1924). A laboratory study of fear: The case of Peter. *The Journal of Genetic Psychology*, 31, 308–315.

Koch, T. & Denike, K. (2006). Rethinking John Snow's South London study: A Bayesian evaluation and recalculation. *Social Science & Medicine*, 63(1), 271–283.

Lynd, R. S. & Lynd, H. M. (1929). *Middletown; a Study in Contemporary American Culture*. New York: Harcourt Brace.

(1937). *Middletown in Transition: A Study in Cultural Conflicts*. New York: Harcourt Brace.

Miles, M. B. & Huberman, M. (1994). *Qualitative Data Analysis*. Thousand Oaks: Sage.

Mill, J. S. (1875). *A System of Logic, Ratiocinative and Inductive: Being a Connected View of the Principles of Evidence and the Methods of Scientific Investigation*. London: Longmans, Green, Reader and Dyer.

Mohr, L. (1982). *Explaining Organizational Behavior*. San Francisco: Jossey-Bass.

Patton, M. Q. (2002). *Qualitative Research & Evaluation Methods*, 3rd ed. Thousand Oaks: Sage.

Presdee, M. (2003). *Cultural Criminology and the Carnival of Crime*. London: Routledge.

Putnam, R. (1993). *Making Democracy Work: Civic Traditions in Modern Italy*. Princeton: Princeton University Press.

Ragin, C. (1992). "Casing" and the process of social inquiry. In C. Ragin & H. Becker (eds.) *What Is a Case? Exploring the Foundations of Social Inquiry*. Cambridge: Cambridge University Press, 217–226.

Rihoux, B. & Ragin, C. C. (2008). *Configurational Comparative Methods: Qualitative Comparative Analysis (QCA) and Related Techniques*. Thousand Oaks: Sage.

Seawright, J. & Gerring, J. (2008). Case selection techniques in case study research: A menu of qualitative and quantitative options. *Political Research Quarterly*, 61(2), 294–308.

Skocpol, T. (1979). *States and Social Revolutions: A Comparative Analysis of France, Russia and China*. Cambridge: Cambridge University Press.

Slater, D. & Ziblatt, D. (2013). The enduring indispensability of the controlled comparison. *Comparative Political Studies*, 46(10), 1301–1327.

Stake, R. E. (1995). *The Art of Case Study Research*. Thousand Oaks: Sage.

Strauss, A. & Corbin, J. M. (1998). *Basics of Qualitative Research: Techniques and Procedures for Developing Grounded Theory*. London: Sage.

Vuori, T. O. & Huy, Q. N. (2016). Distributed attention and shared emotions in the innovation process: How Nokia lost the smartphone battle. *Administrative Science Quarterly*, 61(1), 9–51.

Welch, C., Rumyantseva, M. & Hewerdine, L. J. (2016). Using case research to reconstruct concepts: A methodology and illustration. *Organizational Research Methods*, 19(1), 111–130.

Yin, R. K. (2013). *Case Study Research: Design and Methods.* Thousand Oaks: Sage.

Zielinski, S. (2010, August 18). Cholera, John Snow and the grand experiment. *Smithsonian Magazine.* Available at: www.smithsonianmag.com/science-nature/cholera-john-snow-and-the-grand-experiment-33494689/ (last accessed July 19, 2022).

CHAPTER 6

Do It Again (and Again)
Multiple Embedded Case Study Design

6.1 Exploring Multiple Embedded Case Studies

Imagine yourself as a researcher who is keen on understanding, from a social science perspective, factors that trigger the spread of a pandemic. The first behemoth task that you undertake will be to define the term "pandemic" and the criteria under which an outbreak of a disease would qualify as a pandemic. Once this is taken care of, the next step is to select the cases that would encapsulate the phenomenon of interest. As a keen social science researcher, with a keen pair of eyes we must add, you purposefully sample (remember we discussed this in Chapter 5) two outbreaks that turned into pandemics – the Spanish flu pandemic and the COVID-19 pandemic. What is your case study design here? Well up till now we are still in a multiple holistic design (as discussed in detail in Chapter 4). How can we turn this into a multiple embedded case study design then? For that you need to select embedded units within the selected case, very much like the single embedded case study design (as discussed in Chapter 5). This can be done, for example, for studying the social impact of the two pandemics. The researcher can focus on two temporally embedded units (i.e. before and after the pandemic) within two separate cases (i.e. Spanish flu and COVID-19). The purposeful (theoretical) selection of these two temporal embedded units within two separate cases lands you into a multiple embedded case study design.

The fact that this design has more than one case and multiple embedded units allows it to leverage another layer of comparative analysis that is not possible with the other designs. The single holistic design, by virtue of it being a single "unembedded" case, is handicapped from undertaking any comparative analysis. While this is not the case for the single embedded design, in which within-case comparisons between embedded units are possible, it however, is incapable of conducting between-case comparisons. On the other hand, the multiple holistic design can leverage between-case comparisons. However, due to the absence of embedded units, within-case comparisons are not possible for this design (which is a shame, given the additional, "natural," control such within-case comparisons afford, as discussed in Chapter 5). In this regard, the multiple embedded design is capable of undertaking both within-case comparisons as well as between-cases comparisons – we can compare again (and again). As such, this design can leverage the strengths of both the single embedded and multiple holistic case study designs. Where there is light, there is shade as they say, so this also adds more complexity on how this design can be executed in a rigorous (trustworthy) fashion, especially in terms of "purposefully" selecting the right cases and embedded units, and in terms of choosing the level of analysis (within-case versus across-case).

BUT BEFORE WE MOVE ON, LET'S THINK ABOUT …

… DESIGN DISTINCTIONS BETWEEN THE MULTIPLE EMBEDDED CASE STUDY DESIGN, AND THE SINGLE HOLISTIC, MULTIPLE HOLISTIC AND SINGLE EMBEDDED CASE STUDY DESIGNS

Take a look at this thinking exercise.

Q. Think carefully about what you have read about the multiple embedded case study design. Using your imaginative curiosity, how do you think the multiple embedded case study design is distinct from the following case study designs?

  (i)   Single holistic case study design
  (ii) Multiple holistic case study design
  (iii) Single embedded case study design

List down as many differences as you can think of.

Let us now look in more detail at what makes the multiple embedded case study design distinct and see the design distinctions more explicitly.

6.2 What Makes a Multiple Embedded Case Study Design Distinct?

This design is distinctive in its ability to have more than one level of analysis as well as more than one case, and consequently its capacity to undertake between- and within-case comparisons simultaneously via replication. We discuss each one of them in detail in subsequent subsections.

6.2.1   Multiple Level of Analysis and More than One Case

The level of analysis (as already indicated in Chapter 5) is the level on which the researcher undertakes theory building and, as such, cases and embedded units lie on these different levels. At the end it is the level on which cases (and let us emphasize again, "cases") reside that will determine the design of the case study. In the multiple embedded design, there are two levels of analysis. On one level reside the cases, whereas on the second level embedded units are present.

Moreover, the nature of your level of analysis, very much like your cases and embedded units (again, see Chapter 5), will vary according to your disciplinary leaning. Hence here we don't want to propose a rule of thumb. Rather, we ask you to refer to your research question, which will provide the necessary guidance on the nature of your levels of analysis.

BUT BEFORE WE MOVE ON, LET'S THINK ABOUT ...

... WHAT THESE TWO DIFFERENT LEVELS OF ANALYSIS ARE FOR THE MULTIPLE EMBEDDED DESIGN

For this thinking exercise, we take inspiration from the fictional "Harry Potter" book series (Rowling, 2015). There are no spoilers per se, and you don't require any additional information for this thinking exercise, except that you should be prepared for some magic!

Wingardium Leviosa!
Imagine you are working in the educational department of the Ministry of Magic, and you want to understand how the four houses at Hogwarts School of Witchcraft and Wizardry (i.e. Gryffindor, Hufflepuff, Ravenclaw, and Slytherin) perform in magic exams. You are clearly interested in saying something about the four houses at Hogwarts (a school for magic), but you then decide that it is also important to compare the four houses on three different magic-related exams, namely Ordinary Wizarding Level (O.W.L.), Nastily Exhausting Wizarding Test Level (N.E.W.T.), and the Wizards' Ordinary Magic and Basic Aptitude Test (W.O.M.B.A.T.). Your objects of interest are the four different houses as well as the three separate exams. See Figure 6.1 for a pictorial depiction of the houses and the exams.

Q.1   What are your cases and embedded units?
Q.2   Using the above example, propose a possible single holistic, multiple holistic, and single embedded case study design. Explain and justify.

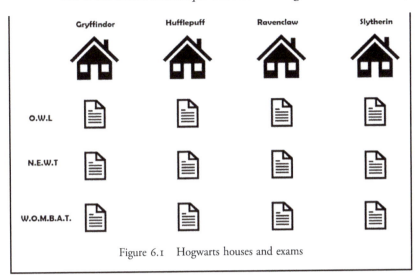

Figure 6.1 Hogwarts houses and exams

BUT SOMEONE TOLD ME THAT ...

... YOU CAN HAVE MORE THAN TWO LEVELS OF ANALYSIS

Can you?

It is possible to have more than two levels of analysis within the multiple embedded design. For example, like Theda Skocpol (1979), a researcher might be interested in social revolutions. For examining social revolutions, the researcher needs to select different countries. However, you can keep on adding further layers of analysis by looking at different cities in those countries that were affected the most by the social revolution. Further granularity can be added by looking at communities within these different cities that were most impacted by the social revolution. In conclusion, theoretically, there is no real restriction on how many levels of analysis can be added to a particular design. If we can move deeper and deeper into further layers of analysis, the thickness of our data will increase. However, this is not always pragmatic given the restrictions on time, availability of data, and other practical concerns.

6.2.2 Between-Case and within-Case Comparisons

Another distinct aspect of this design is its capacity to undertake comparative analysis, namely between- and within-case comparisons. In fact, we can say with affirmation that this is the only design in which you as a

Table 6.1 *Comparisons within-case and between-case for different case study designs*

	Single holistic design	Single embedded design	Multiple holistic design	Multiple embedded design
Comparison within-case	✕	✔		✔
Comparison between-cases	✕		✔	✔

researcher can simultaneously undertake both types of comparative analysis (see Table 6.1).

Comparisons between-cases occur when you juxtapose different and/or similar cases at the level of the case. Let us come back to the social revolution example discussed previously. Since you are interested in social revolutions, you may decide to undertake theoretical replication by selecting two sets of countries. You compare a country that has experienced a social revolution (e.g. France) with another country that has not experienced any social revolution (e.g. United Kingdom). We call such comparisons "between-cases comparison."

BUT BEFORE WE MOVE ON, LET'S THINK ABOUT …

… LITERAL REPLICATION FOR BETWEEN-CASES COMPARISON FOR THE SOCIAL REVOLUTION EXAMPLE

Q. What kind of countries will you have to select here? Explain and justify.

What makes the multiple embedded design so unique is its capacity to undertake comparison within-case as well. This means that, after selecting two set of different countries, you will not stop here! (You would have stopped for a multiple holistic case study design). In fact, you will now undertake within-case comparisons, in which you will select embedded units within-case, with the sole purpose of further investigating your selected cases. For instance, in our social revolution example after undertaking theoretical replication between-cases, you decide to select cities that were affected by the revolution, as this will add to your understanding of the social revolution for the countries you selected.

This added layer of level of analysis, more specifically for embedded units, will turn your design from a multiple holistic to a multiple embedded case study design.

Likewise, for the field of psychology, we relay the thought process of the multiple embedded case study design. We take inspiration from the "marshmallow experiment" conducted by psychologist Walter Mischel at Stanford University (Mischel et al., 1972; Posada, 2009), as well as the counter criticism that his experiment has received (see Resnick, 2018; Watts et al., 2018). Hereafter, we will refer to this example as the "marshmallow" example. As a psychologist you are interested in understanding "delayed gratification," which the APA Dictionary of Psychology defines as "forgoing immediate reward in order to obtain a larger, more desired, or more pleasurable reward in the future."[1] Your interest is not only to understand "delayed gratification" but the influence of income levels on "delayed gratification." Given these considerations you theoretically sample two neighborhoods, one being a rich neighborhood (i.e. income levels in this neighborhood are higher than the average income) and the second being a poor neighborhood (i.e. income levels in this neighborhood are lower than the average income). Convenience sampling also play a role in the selection of these neighborhoods, as they are both in close geographical proximity to where you work. What are the neighborhoods here? Well, the neighborhoods are your two cases. Since you are interested in a multiple embedded case study design, you also need to look within your selected cases. In this regard, you must now decide which age group you are theoretically interested in saying something about. After reading the article "InBrief: The Science of Early Childhood Development" published by the Center on the Developing Child at Harvard University (see Center on the Developing Child, 2007), you "theoretically" sample the age group three to five years old, as this age group represents important years of a child's development. You select 15 children from each neighborhood, and hence now the 30 selected children are your embedded units.[2]

---

[1] https://dictionary.apa.org/delay-of-gratification

[2] It should be noted that children here, apart from being embedded units, are also units of observations (data sources) at the same time.

BUT BEFORE WE MOVE ON, LET'S THINK ABOUT ...

... OTHER POSSIBLE SELECTION STRATEGIES FOR SELECTING YOUR CASES AND
EMBEDDED UNITS

Q. Be imaginative, curious, and think of other possible (hypothetical)
    sampling strategies through which you can select cases and embedded
    units for the "marshmallow" example being discussed here. Explain
    and justify.

So now coming back to our "marshmallow" example, you invite these 30 children to your research institute. To observe "delay of gratification," each child is invited into a room separately. You then place a marshmallow in front of the child and tell him/her that you will leave him/her alone in the room with the marshmallow for 15 minutes. Before leaving the child, you also tell him/her that if the marshmallow is uneaten when you come back, you will reward him/her with another marshmallow. However, if the marshmallow is eaten then you will not reward him/her with another one. You can imagine the restraint needed by the little ones to not eat the marshmallow. Nonetheless, what this set-up represents is an example of multiple embedded design, in which between-cases comparison between neighborhoods and within-case comparison among children are taking place.

Likewise, as a political scientist you might be intrigued by the pictures of the world at night released by NASA Earth Observatory.[3] What strikes you as a political scientist are the visible development differences that emerge in these maps, with the more developed countries shining in all brightness, and the less developed countries (at time) plunging in full darkness. You decide to expound on these visible differences, by providing a theoretical explanation for two regions, namely the Americas and the Korean peninsula. Your aim is to understand why there are differences in economic prosperity within these two regions. To answer your research objective, you select two different countries within each of these regions, namely the United States and Mexico within the Americas and South Korea and North Korea within the Korean Peninsula. So, what do you conclude here? Well, if you were Daron Acemoglu and James Robinson,

---

[3] https://earthobservatory.nasa.gov/images/90008/night-light-maps-open-up-new-applications

you would have likely concluded that differences in economic prosperity between the United States and Mexico within the Americas and South Korea and North Korea within the Korean peninsula are owed to the differences in their political institutions. While both the United States and South Korea have inclusive economic institutions (i.e. institutions that work for the general masses), both Mexico and North Korea have extractive institutions (i.e. non-inclusive institutions that do not work for the general masses) (Robinson & Acemoglu, 2012).

BUT BEFORE WE MOVE ON, LET'S THINK ABOUT . . .

. . . THE CASES AND EMBEDDED UNITS, AND THE KIND OF REPLICATION BEING UNDERTAKEN IN OUR PREVIOUS EXAMPLE

Q.1 Indicate what are the cases and embedded units. Explain and justify.
Q.2 Indicate what kind of replication is taking place for between-case and within-case comaparisons. Explain and justify.
Q.3 Using the jigsaw visual representation provided in Chapter 5, can you provide a similar visual representation for this example?

We provide a jigsaw visual representation of the example discussed in Figure 6.2. As you can see, you have two cases and are undertaking between-cases comparison in the Americas and Korean peninsula. The United States and Mexico are the two embedded units within your Americas case, whereas South and North Korea are the two embedded units within your Korean peninsula case. Now the next big question is, what kind of replication is happening for between-case and within-case comparisons? Well, for between-cases the replication is literal, as we are selecting cases that are the same on the independent and dependent variables. On the other hand, for within-case comparisons, a theoretical replication is being undertaken, since the independent and dependent variables for embedded units within the case vary/differ.

6.3 When Should You Opt for the Multiple Embedded Design?

There is no straightforward answer, but it all boils down to your all-important research question (which we already discussed in Chapter 2). Normally, a multiple embedded design should be used when the intent is to undertake comparative analysis between-cases as well as within-case so as to understand the phenomenon of interest. However, you also need to

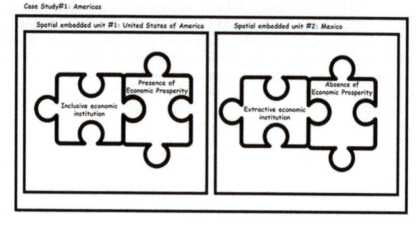

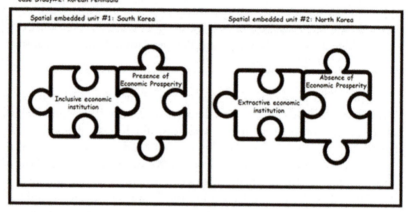

Figure 6.2   Jigsaw visual representation for the example on the Americas and the Korean peninsula

bear in mind that undertaking between- and within-case comparisons "complexifies" the design even further, primarily because you have to decide what kind of between-case and within-case comparisons you want to undertake. Are you undertaking literal and/or theoretical replication for between-case comparison? Are you undertaking literal and/or theoretical replication within-case? As such, this leaves you with many possibilities in which you can design your multiple embedded case study.

BUT BEFORE WE MOVE ON, LET'S THINK ABOUT . . .

. . . DESIGNING A MULTIPLE EMBEDDED CASE STUDY

Indeed, we should! For this thinking exercise we provide a hypothetical research scenario.

Research Scenario #1

When China hosted the 2008 Olympics in Beijing, one of the tasks that the government undertook was improving Beijing's air quality. This was ensured via a series of interventions, for example, by closing factories that were near Beijing (see Yardley, 2008). As a social science researcher, you are interested in understanding the impact of this governmental decision (i.e. of closing factories) on the livelihood of nearby communities. Think about the following questions.

Q.1　What should be the cases and embedded units for your design to be a multiple embedded case study design? Explain and justify.

Q.2　Given your choice of cases and embedded units, what kind of replication (i.e. literal/theoretical) is taking place in the between-case and within-case comparisons?

Of course, there is no right or wrong answer here. One possible way of designing the multiple embedded case study design using this hypothetical research scenario is to treat the communities as your cases. To introduce embedded units within the selected cases, you can look at the communities before and after the governmental decision. Since all the selected communities had experienced a loss of livelihood upon the closure of factories, we can conclude that a literal replication has been undertaken between-cases. On the other hand, since there is variation on the variables of interest within each case, we can conclude that theoretical replication was undertaken here.

BUT BEFORE WE MOVE ON, LET'S THINK ONCE MORE ABOUT . . .

. . . DESIGNING A MULTIPLE EMBEDDED CASE STUDY DESIGN!

Again, here is a hypothetical research scenario.

As an environmental researcher, you are interested in understanding the impact of oil spills on the environment. Given the aim of your research, you purposeful select two similar companies, which are British Petroleum and Royal Dutch Shell Oil. Both these companies have experienced oil spills.

Let's take a pause here and think about the following:

Q.1   What kind of replication is taking place for between-cases comparison (i.e. is it literal and/or theoretical)?

Q.2   What kind of embedded units can you select here? Don't forget to be imaginatively curious!

Given that both oil companies experienced oil spills, we would contend that a literal replication was undertaken for between-cases comparison. Regarding what kind of embedded units can be selected, here there could be many different possibilities. One being the treatment of oil spillage incidents as embedded units within both companies. For example, for British Petroleum you may decide to look into the incidents of "Port Bonython oil spill" that occurred in the south of Australia in 1992, as well as the more recent "Deepwater Horizon oil spill" that occurred at the Gulf of Mexico in 2010. For Royal Dutch Shell Oil you may decide to select the oil spillages in Nigeria in 2001 and 2008. So, what kind of replication is this? Again, it boils down to whether there are any theoretical differences among these embedded units and, since all these four incidents negatively affected the environment, we can consider this as literal replication within-case. For a visual representation, see Figure 6.3.

We now conclude this section and provide a little sneak peek into what is to come in Chapters 7 and 8, by providing an example inspired by Angrist and Lavy's (1999) article on class size and scholastic achievement. Let's imagine you are an educational researcher who is interested in unpacking the relationship between class size and test scores of students. One way to approach this problem could be by first purposefully sampling two or more schools. For our purposes let's stick to two schools – School A and School B. You purposefully select them because School A has large class sizes (i.e. the number of students is over 25 in each class), whereas School B has small class sizes (i.e. the number of students is less than 25 in each class). What kind of replication is this? Well, you as the researcher are undertaking theoretical replication between-cases, since the two schools differ on the independent variable class size. Let's say, if you decide to analyze only these two cases then what kind of design is this? We have a multiple holistic case study design. Now, let's assume that, after conducting some field observations and preliminary interviews, you identify that both schools have three different sections of kindergarten. Given the importance that educational and psychological literature puts on early year education, you decide that it is important for theory building purposes to

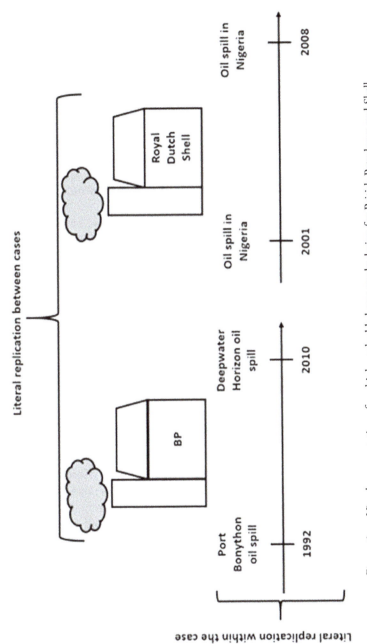

Figure 6.3 Visual representation of multiple embedded case study design for British Petroleum and Shell

introduce another level of analysis within the case, which is at the level of the kindergarten class. Your insights make you revise the aim of your research to unpack the relationship between class size and test scores of students for early school year education. Since there are no theoretical differences among these three kindergarten sections within each school, you are primarily undertaking a literal replication, in which the selected kindergarten sections are your "embedded units." By being imaginatively curious, you have followed up on your insights and did not hesitate in changing your design from a multiple holistic to a multiple embedded case study design. This malleable capacity of case study design is what we refer to as a sequencing case study design. But as we already said this is just a sneak peek, and we will discuss this in more detail in Chapters 7 and 8.

For now, let us discuss more specifically the design strengths and weaknesses for the multiple embedded case study design. While there will be some repetitions from the weaknesses indicated in Chapter 4 on multiple holistic design, we feel it is important to discuss them here in the context of multiple embedded designs.

6.4   Strengths and Weaknesses

6.4.1   Strength #1: Increased Internal Validity through Comparative Analysis between- and within-Cases

A key strength of this design is that it is capable of undertaking comparisons not only within the case, as it is for the single embedded design, but also between-cases. This design therefore has more than one "level of analysis," which allows it to leverage the strengths of comparative analysis not only at the level of the case, but also within the case. Moreover, given that there are between-case and within-case comparisons taking place, the researcher can leverage replication for these two different comparative modes. As already indicated in Chapter 4, replication, and more specifically between-case theoretical replication, strengthens internal validity of the causal claims that a researcher makes. However, beyond using replication at the case level, the researcher can also use theoretical replication within the case to probe the full spectrum of variation (as discussed in Chapter 5). This was evident in the "marshmallow" example as well as the Americas and Korean peninsula example, in which theoretical replication between-case, but also within-case, allowed the internal validity of the concerned case study to be strengthened.

BUT SOMEONE TOLD ME *AGAIN* THAT . . .

... YOU CAN ALSO STRENGTHEN GENERALIZABILITY (A.K.A. EXTERNAL VALIDITY) IF
YOU USE A MULTIPLE EMBEDDED DESIGN

Is that so?

Yes, it could strengthen generalizability. But the big question is, how does it strengthen generalizability? Before answering this question, let us discuss Hallen and Eisenhardt's (2012) paper which explored "how firms efficiently form interorganizational ties" (p. 38). To answer this research question, the researchers opted for a multiple embedded design. To justify the use of this design, the authors indicate the following in the paper. "Given limited theory and evidence for how firms efficiently form ties, we used inductive theory building with embedded multiple cases. Multiple cases enable building more robust, generalizable, and parsimonious theory than single cases. Our embedded design has several levels of analysis (i.e. round and venture) to improve the likelihood of rich and accurate theory" (p. 38). As this quote succinctly explains, beyond the usefulness of the multiple embedded design for theory building, they also see the design being helpful for providing "more" generalizable results, when compared to the single case study design. Therefore, the multiple embedded case study design, given its capacity to undertake theoretical and literal replication between-case and within-case, enhances the generalizing capacity of this design.

6.4.2 Strength #2: Offers a Variety of Different Design Possibilities

Another strength of the multiple embedded design is that researchers can opt for various designs, which is not possible with other case study designs. We did highlight this very explicitly in Section 6.1, but we recap it here again. This strength is due to the reason that both between-case and within-case comparisons are possible in this design. Given these possibilities, the researcher has more options regarding the ways in which he/she can recombine literal and/or theoretical replication between-cases with literal and/or theoretical replication within-cases. Consequently, the multitude of options in which these considerations can be recombined provides the researcher the necessary flexibility to opt for a design that suits his/her research needs (see Table 6.2).

Of course, the next question you might have is regarding how to decide which kind of replication you should take for between-case and within-case comparisons? Well, by now we think you would know our answer, and that is it all boils down to your black hole, which is what? Yes, you are right. It is your research question!

Table 6.2 *Design consideration for multiple embedded case study design*

		What kind of replication do you want to undertake?
Design Consideration	Comparisons between the cases	☐ Theoretical ☐ Literal ☐ Theoretical & Literal
	Comparisons within the cases	☐ Theoretical ☐ Literal ☐ Theoretical & Literal

6.4.3   Weakness #1: Lack of Contextual Depth-Can Only Focus on a Small Number of Explanatory Variables (or Constructs)

This design, by virtue of having more than one case and embedded units, makes it difficult to interrogate contextual depth, primarily because comparisons are being undertaken between and within cases to either indicate differences or similarities on the variables of interest. Such comparisons on the variables of interest can only be meaningful when context is not discussed in-depth. If the researcher still wishes to engage with the context, he/she might face the risk of getting lost in a myriad of explanatory variables, even those that are of no interest to the researcher herself (or himself). This will make the comparative analysis more challenging. Hence, any meaningful comparisons can only be done at the expense of compromising on deep contextual explanations.

6.4.4   Weakness #2: Access to the Cases and Embedded Units Can Be Difficult to Get

Given that there is more than one case and embedded unit in the multiple embedded design, access to the main and embedded units can be difficult to negotiate. Of course, the issue of access is also relevant for the single holistic, single embedded, and multiple holistic designs. But, given there are more units (i.e. cases and embedded units) to consider for the multiple embedded design, getting access to all the relevant units (i.e. cases and embedded units) can be particularly difficult to achieve. For example, in the field of International Business, Chandra (2017), who explored entrepreneurs' evaluations of international entrepreneurial opportunities (IEOs) and the role of time in the evaluation process, highlights the issue of access.

The author first indicates the use of theoretical sampling for selecting the cases, through the following passage.

> For this study's theoretical sampling, I selected cases that were early internationalizers, i.e., those internationalizing within 6 years after inception; and assessed whether and how their evaluation of early and late-stage IEOs differed, and why. I selected the cases from a pool of SMEs based in Australia using business and government directories (i.e., Kompass database, Australian Technology Showcase, Australian Trade Commission), three leading Australian business magazines, Business Review Weekly, Australian Business Solutions, Business First Magazine, and three major Australian newspapers, The Australian, Sydney Morning Herald, Australian Financial Review. (p. 429)

However, he further indicates that "Of the 60 firms contacted from the firm database described above, 15 firms responded positively and became the focus of this study" (p. 429). This is of course nothing new for a qualitative researcher (and in fact even for quantitative folks). Researchers are familiar with situations in which access to a particular organization/firm/institution might be refused. But this example is an important reminder that access is not always easy to get, and hence should be considered if you wish to adopt a multiple embedded case study design in your study.

6.5 Brief Summary

The multiple embedded case study design has both merits as well as demerits. We summarize the key strengths along with weaknesses here and indicate them in our Case Checklist in Table 6.3.

- The first strength is that the internal validity of this design is high because the design is capable of undertaking both between-case and within-case comparisons. Consequently, this allows the design to leverage replication when comparisons are being undertaken between- and within-cases.
- The second strength of the multiple embedded design is its capacity to offer multiple design possibilities. Given that different kinds of replications (i.e. literal and/or theoretical) can be undertaken for both between- and within-case comparisons, a number of options in which these considerations can be recombined are available for the researcher to consider.
- The first weakness is that this design is unable to provide in-depth contextualized explanations. Therefore, in comparison to some other designs, this design is unable to provide contextual depth.

Table 6.3 *Checklist table on the strengths and weakness of case study designs*

Type of Case Study Design		Strengths	Weaknesses
Archetypical case study designs	Single Holistic	□ Fine grained explanatory power (explain a process) □ Falsification □ Data access and construct validity □ Unlimited variables	□ Internal validity (because can't undertake variance analysis) □ External validity (can't generalize findings to a population of cases)
	Multiple Holistic	□ Undertake literal replication (enhances reliability) □ Undertake theoretical replication (enhances internal validity) □ Undertake theoretical replication (enhances external validity)	□ Depth of observation is compromised □ Difficult to control for context (given that we cannot manipulate) □ Additional independent variable exponentially increases the complexity of research design
	Single Embedded	□ Higher internal validity (compared to single holistic and LR multiple holistic case study designs) □ TR single embedded design has a higher external validity (compared to the single holistic design and to LR in a multiple holistic design)	□ Smaller number of explanatory variables (when compared to the single holistic case study design) □ External validity of a TR single embedded design will be lower than a TR multiple case study design
	Multiple Embedded	□ Increased internal validity through comparative analysis between-case and within-case □ Offers a variety of different designs	□ Lack of contextual depth □ Difficult to get access to all the selected cases and embedded units

- The second weakness is acquiring the necessary access to the selected cases and embedded units. This can be a practical issue and, as such, negotiating access to all the selected cases and embedded units can be difficult.

REFERENCES

Angrist, J. D. & Lavy, V. (1999). Using Maimonides' rule to estimate the effect of class size on scholastic achievement. *The Quarterly Journal of Economics*, 114 (2), 533–575.

Center on the Developing Child. (2007). *InBrief: The Science of Early Childhood Development.* Available at: https://developingchild.harvard.edu/resources/inbrief-science-of-ecd/ (last accessed July 19, 2022)

Chandra, Y. (2017). A time-based process model of international entrepreneurial opportunity evaluation. *Journal of International Business Studies*, 48(4), 423–451.

Hallen, B. L. & Eisenhardt, K. M. (2012). Catalyzing strategies and efficient tie formation: How entrepreneurial firms obtain investment ties. *Academy of Management Journal*, 55(1), 35–70.

Mischel, W., Ebbesen, E. B., & Raskoff Zeiss, A. (1972). Cognitive and attentional mechanisms in delay of gratification. *Journal of Personality and Social Psychology*, 21(2), 204–218.

Posada, J. D. (2009, February 24). Don't eat the marshmallow! *TED Talks.* Available at: www.ted.com/talks/joachim_de_posada_don_t_eat_the_marshmallow?language=en (last accessed July 19, 2022).

Resnick, B. (2018, June 6). The "marshmallow test" said patience was a key to success. A new replication tells us s'more. *Vox.* Available at: www.vox.com/science-and-health/2018/6/6/17413000/marshmallow-test-replication-mischel-psychology#:~:text=Share%20All%20sharing%20options%20for,replication%20tells%20us%20s'more.&text=Here's%20some%20good%20news%3A%20Your,minutes%20to%20get%20two%20marshmallows (last accessed July 19, 2022).

Robinson, J. A. & Acemoglu, D. (2012). *Why Nations Fail: The Origins of Power, Prosperity and Poverty.* London: Profile.

Rowling, J. K. (2015). *Harry Potter and the Philosopher's Stone.* London: Bloomsbury Publishing.

Skocpol, T. (1979). *States and Social Revolutions: A Comparative Analysis of France, Russia and China.* Cambridge: Cambridge University Press.

Watts, T. W., Duncan, G. J. & Quan, H. (2018). Revisiting the marshmallow test: A conceptual replication investigating links between early delay of gratification and later outcomes. *Psychological Science*, 29(7), 1159–1177.

Yardley, J. (2008, July 7). Cities near Beijing close factories to improve air for Olympics. *The New York Times.* Available at: www.nytimes.com/2008/07/07/sports/olympics/07china.html#:~:text=BEIJING%20%E2%80%94%20With%20Beijing%20struggling%20to,Games%2C%20state%20news%20media%20reported (last accessed July 19, 2022).

CHAPTER 7

Sequencing Case Study Designs
Inductive–Deductive

7.1 Introducing the Sequencing Case Study Design

Charles Darwin was an exceptional researcher of his time, and his proposed theory of evolution was revolutionary in the field of biology. While most would appreciate his contribution to science, what made him special as a researcher was his tenacity to engage with his imaginative curiosity! Yes, you heard us right, imaginative curiosity. We have in fact used the phrase "imaginative curiosity" quite often throughout the book. Can you tell us what it means to you? Well, let us discuss our take on it by digging into the research life of Charles Darwin (here on we will refer to him as Charles).

Charles was born in 1809 and from a young age he was interested in reading and exploring nature. In 1831, he accepted an offer to travel on the HMS *Beagle* that navigated around the world for five years. During his trips he took extensive field notes and collected different types of fauna, flora, and even fossil specimens (as evidence). In short, like a true qualitative researcher, he did not shy away from observing and immersing himself completely whilst making sure that the "richness" of these observations were recorded extensively. However, what we would like to discuss more specifically, was Charles's trip to the Galapagos islands. This trip was after Charles had traveled and observed the South America's mainland coastline. The Galapagos Islands, unlike South America's mainland, were constituted by isolated volcanic islands (Sulloway, 2005) and lay 600 miles away from Ecuador (Lack, 1983). The HMS beagle went on to make a five-week voyage through the Galapagos islands, and it was here that Charles noticed some important differences among different species. For example, he noticed that islands were inhabited by finches (small-to-medium-sized songbirds) that were similar to the mainland finches. Yet, while bearing similarities, these island finches were not completely similar to the mainland finches. What was even more revealing were the differences present among the same species of finches on the different islands.

For example, finches on one island had beaks well adapted to eat nuts or seeds, while those on another island had beaks that were more suited for eating insects (Meijer, 2018; Podos, 2001). This observation allowed Charles to infer that, whilst the finches on the islands had a common ancestor (who likely came from mainland South America), each of the different sub-species of finches had adapted to the varying environmental conditions of the different islands. These (among many other) observations went on to provide the foundation on which Charles proposed his theory of evolution.

Now, let's put the above story in the context of designing a case study, and perhaps even let us imagine (for a brief moment) that you were Charles Darwin setting foot in Town A on the mainland coastline of South America. In this fictional example inspired by real events, let us imagine that you noticed finches, and your interest was to provide "new explanations" for the finches living in Town A. To achieve this objective you recorded their structure, amount of plumage, beak size and shape, as well as eating and other social habits. During this very rich analysis, you realized that no additional information was coming in. What could you have done? Well if you had stopped your investigation at this point, your study would have been an inductive single holistic case study in which Town A is the case. This is where being imaginatively curious becomes fundamental from falling short in making not just "a contribution" but an "impactful contribution."

As we learn from Charles Darwin himself, his trip to the Galapagos Islands was instrumental in gathering the needed information for his theory of evolution. So, if you had stopped at Town A, you might as well have stopped yourself from providing a potentially groundbreaking insight in your theory. In this regard it is your imaginative curiosity that would have led you to where you need to go next and, lo and behold, it took you to the Galapagos islands. So, what did you just do here? Well, you engaged in sequencing your case study design! This is because, while you had started with a single holistic design with Town A, later on you became interested in the Galapagos islands. If we consider the individual islands as the cases, what you conducted was a multiple holistic case study. In short you sequenced your case study design and transformed it from a single holistic to a multiple holistic case study design. What this means is that as a researcher, even when it feels like you have met the objective of your research, being imaginatively curious to seek and learn more is likely to provide more theoretical insights. From this vantage point, this would simply mean that if there were more islands to explore, you should have investigated them as well.

So, in short, what can we learn from Charles Darwin's research life? Well, most fundamentally, we learn about his willingness to be relentlessly inquisitive (Nicholls, 2017). It was his tenacity to being curious and imaginative that allowed Charles to postulate a very powerful, novel, and impactful theory. And, while it may require more time, it is this willingness to follow up and investigate that can put you a step closer to making a meaningful theoretical contribution to your discipline.

7.2   So, What Is Sequencing Case Study Design? Let's Dive in!

In this book so far, we have described individual archetypical case study designs, depending on whether single or multiple cases are used and whether there are embedded units inside the case(s). Indeed, as a qualitative researcher you must have heard the dreaded four words "what is your contribution?" during the review/dissertation process. To hopefully answer this dreaded question, we invite our readers to be imaginatively curious! As explained earlier, it is the tenacity and willingness to be unapologetically inquisitive that helps you to spot some of the most interesting and groundbreaking insights. So how does "imaginative curiosity" look in the case of case study designs? For one, we can start by not viewing the archetypical case study designs as static standalones, but rather as dynamic and malleable designs. We can acknowledge that these archetypical case study designs can be (re)combined in many different ways to suit our research purpose. This recombination is what we call *sequencing case study designs*. So, what are the benefits of sequencing case study designs? Unfortunately, there are not many research studies that engage with sequencing case study designs, and as such we will provide some illustration, by diving more deeply later into one exemplar study by Doz (1996). Through this illustration, we will explain the process and the benefits of sequencing case study designs for your own research purpose. Before going deep into the Doz study, let us come back to our question: What are the benefits of sequencing case study designs? Allow us to illustrate this with the help of a paper by Magnani and Zucchella (2019).

Magnani and Zucchella (2019) were interested in understanding entrepreneurial ventures and how they cope with uncertainty. Via criterion (purposeful) sampling they identified nine firms (cases). Each of these nine firms were similar to one another. In the authors' own words:

> In the first stage, we sampled firms according to the following criteria: first, manufacturing firms originating in Italy were chosen to be the initial

context focus of the study to gather knowledge about international smaller firms. Second, each firm had to have less than 500 employees and therefore qualify as smaller firm ... Third, each firm had to be already internationalised or within its internationalisation process. Pre-internationalised firms were particularly insightful because they allowed us to interview decision makers who were starting the foreign expansion. Fourth, each firm had to show entrepreneurial features either in terms of enduring international growth, as in the case of old born globals, or in their proactive pursuit of opportunities for growth, as in the case of younger firms. (p. 134)

Now, they could have stopped here if they wanted to, but they went on to add one further case in order to confirm or disconfirm their preliminary findings. To do so, they introduced "sector variation in the sample (services) and country of origin (different than Italy)" (p. 134). We can say that Magnani and Zucchella (2019) were sequencing their case study design by first engaging in a multiple holistic design, followed by a single holistic design. So, what is the benefit? As discussed in Section 7.1, sequencing case study designs can help you in proposing a more comprehensive theory. We are not saying that the archetypical case study designs on their own are not useful and do not add value. As already discussed at length in this book, these individual standalone designs are important. However, in this book we want to acknowledge that these archetypical designs also come with weaknesses despite their strengths. These weaknesses can be addressed by sequencing case study designs which will allow the researcher to draw on the advantages of each standalone design while overcoming their individual shortcomings.

To illustrate this better, we come back to our example of Charles's research. If you remember, we said that Charles began his research with a single holistic design with one case, that is Town A. We must ask ourselves here – what are the advantages of using a single holistic case study design? The undeniable strength of this design is that it constitutes the most flexible and the most exploratory case study design which allows the inclusion of myriad explanatory variables. Consequently, by using the single holistic case study design, Charles collected in-depth and rich contextual information on the finches, which might have been difficult to achieve with other case study designs. It is therefore not very surprising to see why the single holistic case study design might be well-suited at the beginning of a sequence. This can subsequently be followed by another design (e.g. single embedded, multiple holistic, or multiple embedded case study design). In our example, it was the multiple holistic case study design. The rationale here was that the subsequent design was able to overcome the shortcomings of the single holistic (or the earlier design) as it focused on specific, apparently consequential, variables which were examined in a co-variational manner in order to confirm/disconfirm the conclusions from earlier phases. The sequencing of the design, however, is not only limited to the design but is also based on the logical reasoning used. In this example of Charles, the single holistic design was used inductively, precisely because he started with an open "mind." Concurrently, with an open/exploratory research design, slowly but steadily (via a series of studies using within- and/or between-case comparisons), he arrived at more robust conclusions deductively (for a refresher on induction and deduction, see Chapter 2). These conclusions proved to be true in a variety of contexts. Consequently, the sequencing of case study design also hinges on your logical reasoning. In this example, we have an inductive–deductive sequence. Is the inductive–deductive sequencing design abductive, you ask? You are absolutely right!

We can also imagine another abductive approach to sequencing, the deductive–inductive sequence, where we start with a larger sample of cases (i.e. with a multiple holistic or a multiple embedded case study design) and study them in a co-variational manner based on largely pre-defined relationships from our original research question. When and if we find that these relationships do not seem to "hold" in the given sample, that is, when we find outliers, we use it as an opportunity (and a good excuse) to sequence it with a more inductive design. This includes, foremost, the single holistic design. We can probe the idiosyncrasies of the one case we have access to in order to find alternative explanations. Once these patterns become apparent, it is time to go back to the remaining cases, and re-analyze existing data using the newly revealed relationships. But more to come on this in Chapter 8.

BUT SOMEONE ASKED ME ...

... IS SEQUENCING CASE STUDY DESIGN ONLY ABDUCTIVE?
Well not at all! Let us revisit our earlier example of Charles. His use of the single holistic design by inductively analyzing Town A rested on the premise that the intent was to infer "new" explanations. Of course, instead of confirming/disconfirming these insights (i.e. deductively) by following up with a multiple holistic design (the Galapagos islands), the subsequent design could also have been inductive. As such, with the second design, Charles could have inductively sought out new relationships. Similarly, Charles could have also undertaken a deductive–deductive approach. This would have been the case if there was already a well-established explanation on the finches which he

wanted to confirm/disconfirm by studying finches in Town A (single holistic case), followed by a confirmatory/disconfirmatory study on the Galapagos islands (multiple holistic). What we are saying here is that there are endless possibilities when it comes to the different ways in which you can sequence your case study designs.

As discussed in the previous box insert, sequenced case study designs can come in all shapes and sizes. However, there are two important design decisions that you must make when you are sequencing. The first is to decide upon the kind of logical reasoning you want to use, and the second is to decide upon a design that you think will best fit the chosen logical reasoning and your research question. We relay design decisions pertaining to sequencing case studies in Figure 7.1. As evident from the figure, there are endless possibilities with regards to sequencing, and there is no rule of thumb on when you need to stop. This is because every case study is different and, hence, the number of designs that you may have to sequence will vary considerably based on the research field, the research study, etc. But, at the end of the day, it comes down to your own imaginative curiosity. In simple words, you can stop sequencing when the sequence satiates your imaginative curiosity.

BUT SOMEONE ASKED ME . . .

. . .IS SATIATING YOUR "IMAGINATIVE CURIOSITY" THEORETICAL SATURATION? Well yes and no! And before we go on to explain why we think that, let us recollect what theoretical saturation is. As we saw in Chapter 4, theoretical saturation happens when additional data collection adds no "new" theoretical insights (Bloor & Wood, 2006; Corbin & Strauss, 2014). As such, the researcher can hold this as a justification to stop data collection.

Now this brings us to the question – how does theoretical saturation contrast with satiating imaginative curiosity? In spirit, the two are the same as both have the desire to seek out more information until no new information comes in. However, the difference between them lies in the fact that theoretical saturation is applicable only in the realm of data collection, whereas imaginative curiosity lies in the realm of the research design. But, more importantly, imaginative curiosity ensures that the case study design is not a static entity that has to be preconceived before beginning the research process. In fact, you can adjust and tweak the designs as you progress through your research. In short, as a researcher, you should not be afraid to add a new case study design as new insights roll in. It is this yearning to follow up on one's own imaginative curiosity that we would like you to feel for the phenomenon that you are researching!

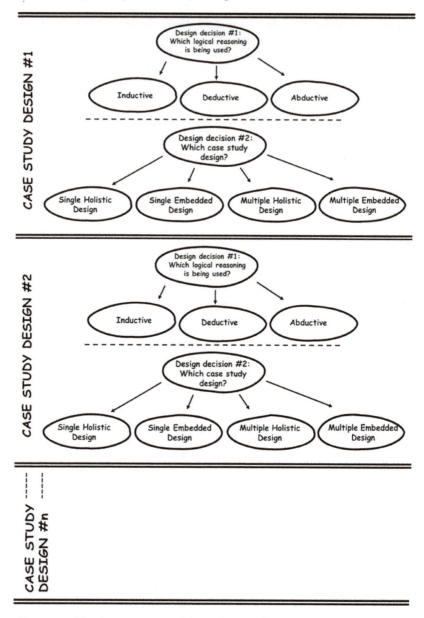

Figure 7.1   Visual representation of design decisions for sequencing case study design

BUT SOMEONE ALSO ASKED ME ...

... IS SEQUENCING CASE STUDY DESIGN AN ITERATIVE PROCESS?

Indeed, it is! Sequencing case study design does not preclude the very essence of qualitative research, which is iterative in nature. Therefore, off we go back and forth between the data and the analysis (Mills et al., 2010; Ritchie et al., 2013), as shown in Figure 7.2.

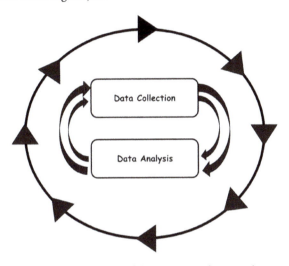

Figure 7.2   Visual representation of the iterative cycles in qualitative research

In fact, we will venture on to say that it is this going back and forth between the data and the analysis that allows the researcher to discover some very compelling and interesting insights. As such, these interesting insights might also motivate the use of another case study design for the research study in hand. Therefore, the iterative cycle of qualitative research (i.e. the going back and forth between the data and analysis) can be present within each case study design and it is this iteration that informs the next steps. We represent this visualization in Figure 7.3.

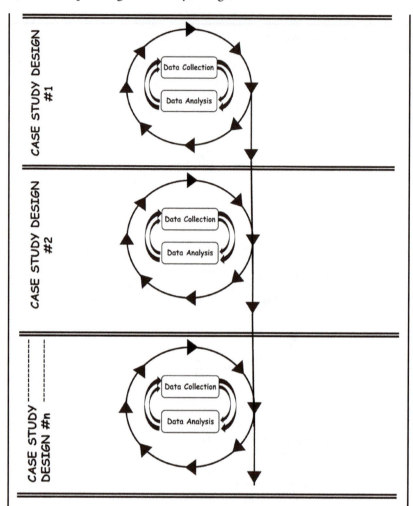

Figure 7.3   Visual representation of the iterative cycles present within sequenced case study designs

BUT BEFORE WE MOVE ON LET'S THINK ABOUT THE ...

... DOZ (1996) PAPER "THE EVOLUTION OF COOPERATION IN STRATEGIC ALLIANCES:
INITIAL CONDITIONS OR LEARNING PROCESSES?"

Read the Doz (1996) paper carefully, and answer the following questions:

Q.1   What is the research question?
Q.2   What are the cases? How are these cases selected?
Q.3   Are there any embedded units? If so, what are they?

Q.4   What are the independent, dependent, and control variables?
Q.5   What case study designs are being used? What are the different levels of analysis?
Q.6   Do you see any sequencing of case study designs? If so, what are they and in which order do they appear?

We hope that you have given some thought to the box insert because, in the rest of the chapter, we will be engaging with the Doz (1996) paper in detail for showcasing one (of the many) ways of sequencing case study designs. By diving deeply into this example, we stay true to the spirit of qualitative research and provide rich in-depth insights on "how" sequencing of case study designs can be undertaken. Moreover, it allows us to display the different design components more explicitly and provide our readers with a concrete example of how to report a sequenced case study.

7.3   Doz (1996) As an Illustrative Example of Sequencing Case Study Designs: Inductive–Deductive

Doz's (1996) study provides an illustrative example of sequencing of case study designs, specifically an inductive–deductive sequencing. The study by Doz emerged as the most rigorous case study in a review of all case study-based articles published in the top 10 management journals (Gibbert et al., 2008). As such, the study provides rich insights into the sequencing of research designs. The study starts inductively with an emphasis on theory building and ends on a deductive, theory-testing mode. It was done in the context of strategic alliances, that is, collaborations between two or more firms to achieve a certain goal (e.g. technology development, market access in a foreign country, etc.). The starting point for Doz was an imbalance in the literature on strategic alliances relative to other literature in management. In particular, the literature on strategic alliances was characterized by a strong focus on the initial characteristics and conditions that lead to an alliance at the expense of evolutionary processes (including learning) that might take place between the partners after the inception of the alliance, and which might (also) influence alliance outcomes. Thus, while initial conditions remain important, evolutionary processes might mediate the initial conditions and jointly influence outcomes. The paper by Doz, therefore, sets out to explore the relative importance of initial conditions versus evolutionary processes in the outcomes of strategic alliances. The abstract provides a glimpse of the individual case studies in the overall sequential design:

> Through a longitudinal case study of two projects in one alliance, replicated and extended in another four projects in two alliances, a framework was developed to analyze the evolution of cooperation in strategic alliances. Successful alliance projects were highly evolutionary and went through a sequence of interactive cycles of learning, reevaluation and readjustment. Failing projects, conversely, were highly inertial, with little learning or divergent learning between cognitive understanding and behavioral adjustment, or frustrated expectations. (Doz, 1996: p. 55)

While Doz (1996) called the overall design a "longitudinal case study," its individual components were far more revealing and need to be appreciated for a full appraisal of the sophistication of that design. As we can see from the previous quotation, there was an initial study of two projects in one alliance, which was followed ("replicated and extended" – more about the "and extended" in due course) by another two alliances with a total of four projects. Now, against the background of the chapters so far, we can disentangle the sequence of the design here: overall there were three case studies of three alliances, each with a number of projects. This suggests that there were three single embedded case studies (i.e. strategic alliances), each with a number of "projects." So, what were these cases and what were the projects?

7.3.1   The First Case Is Ciba Geigy–Alza

The paper explicates:

> Between 1977 and 1982, Alza and Ciba Geigy collaborated in the development of advanced drug delivery system (ADDS) applications, combining Alza's expertise in ADDS and Ciba Geigy's experience of pharmaceutical development, production and marketing. In particular, they worked on two technologies; oral slow-release pills (OROS in short) and transdermal patches (TTS in short). Alza was to do the research and advanced development, Ciba Geigy the registration, production and marketing. Alza was a small entrepreneurial organization based in Palo Alto (California), Ciba Geigy a major chemicals and Pharmaceuticals multinational, based in Basel (Switzerland). (Doz, 1996: p. 57)

7.3.2   The Second Case Is AT&T–Olivetti

The second case focused on a collaboration between AT&T (a telecommunication company) and Olivetti (then a leading Italian supplier of computers and office electronics) between 1983 and 1989. The two projects involved (a) the development of a new UNIX-based range of minicomputers and (b) a new generation of microcomputers. Thus, at the time of the research and following divestiture of the regional telephone operating companies in the United States, AT&T was trying to internationalize its operations and to enter the computer industry and Olivetti provided the needed market access in Europe (Doz, 1996).

7.3.3   The Third Case Is GE–SNECMA

The third case involved General Electric and SNECMA. There were two projects. In the first, the two companies collaborated in the civilian jet engine business. The collaboration started in the 1960s with SNECMA being a minority partner in GE's large engine program (the CF6). This initial project was followed by a second project, that is, a joint program to develop and manufacture a midrange engine, the CFM56, started in 1973 and first commercialized in 1979. SNECMA was a major French manufacturer of aircraft engines. GE was a major manufacturer of turbines and of jet engines for the US military at the beginning of the alliance and has since gained leadership of the US aircraft engine industry from Pratt & Whitney (Doz, 1996).

7.3.4   Components of the Case Study Design

What can we learn from this case study in the context of our second chapter, that is, the one about the components of the research design? As we outlined in Chapters 2, 5, and 6, the main components of a case study design are the research question, the variables (independent, dependent, control), the cases (and embedded units if present), as well as the level of analysis. Let's look at each in turn in the context of the Doz (1996) paper.

7.3.4.1   Research Question

Recall that the research questions can be explanatory and/or exploratory. The main difference here is that the explanatory type focuses explicitly on the effect of some independent variable on the dependent variable, whereas the exploratory type seeks to "describe" a phenomenon again often in terms of the independent/dependent variables, but less explicitly in terms of any causal effect. We also said that explanatory research questions can be subdivided into those that are focused explicitly on the independent variable and those that are instead using the dependent variable as the starting point (see Table 2.1).

Let's see what type of research question we find in Doz's case. The first thing that comes to mind is that the author took a very theory-driven approach in this study. The literature on strategic alliances exhibited an undue focus on initial characteristics (in our case, the independent variable) as determinants of alliance outcomes (the dependent variable). So that pointed out the "gap" in the literature and coincidentally excused Doz for focusing on evolutionary processes (including learning) between the partners which might (also) influence alliance outcomes. Doz did not dismiss the importance of initial conditions but rather proposed to investigate such evolutionary processes jointly with initial conditions. As we suggested in Chapter 2, it is always a good idea to feature the main ingredients of the research design (above all the dependent and independent variables) in the title of the paper. And this is exactly what we find in Doz's case: "The evolution of collaboration in strategic alliances: Initial conditions or learning processes?" In summary, Doz investigated what the (combined) effect of initial conditions and learning processes was on the evolution of collaboration in strategic alliances.

Now, as we can see from the brief discussion in the previous paragraph, the nature of the research question is clearly causal, and as such explanatory. Doz seeks to explain the phenomenon more fully. He explained how the dependent variable (alliance success) is influenced by the interplay of two independent variables, one studied extensively (initial conditions) and one studied far less (learning processes). So clearly the research question here was in the format "What is the effect of X on Y?" or "How does X affect Y?" As the discussion of the prior literature showed, Doz was (of course) interested in the dependent variable, alliance success. But what really intrigued him was the interplay of different types of independent variables, some studied extensively, some outright ignored. So, his explicit emphasis in the theoretical discussion is on the dearth of research regarding learning processes and their role in (also) explaining alliance success (above and beyond initial conditions), which strongly suggests that his research question is X-centered.

What about induction versus deduction in this example? An inductive research question almost by definition is more attractive, as it allows us to come up with novel insights, that is, those that cannot be deduced from prior literature. In other words, inductive research questions are (more) likely to provide much-coveted theoretical contributions. Doz' case is revealing in this regard, as it is both inductive and deductive. Let us explain this: While we know quite a lot about the effect of initial conditions (the deductive element), we know very little about learning processes (the inductive element) and even less about the interplay between learning processes and initial conditions. Thus, the theoretical contribution resides precisely in the inductive starting point, that is, the limited prior knowledge about the effect of learning processes in the context of initial conditions. Far from being an intellectual exercise in pigeonholing different types of research questions, these distinctions are important and have far-reaching consequences for the other elements of the case study design, above all for the approach to theoretical sampling.

7.3.4.2   Theoretical (Purposeful) Sampling

The common denominator in the theoretical sampling decision in Doz's study was to focus on the cases of new business and new product development, even across different industry contexts (ranging from pharmaceutical via office electronics to jet engines). As Doz (1996) noted, such alliances would offer a relatively balanced situation between the two independent variables, initial conditions, and process variables to affect alliance outcomes.

It was a deliberate decision to choose these types of alliances instead of more traditional alliances which had resource access or market entry joint ventures, and in which initial conditions or process variables largely affected outcomes. In other words, Doz sought such alliances where, from the start, both initial conditions and process variables played balanced roles in affecting outcomes. Note that his choice of balancing the potential impact of the two explanatory variables across cases represented a safeguard against selection bias. The cases were not selected from one spectrum of possible outcomes (only), that is, they were not cases in which either initial conditions or learning processes prevailed. Note that without comparing cases across a minimum range of variance, the results might not have been representative of other strategic alliance cases, which exhibit similar characteristics.

Not comparing cases across a minimum range of variance would have reduced the external validity of the study. Even more importantly, the internal validity of selecting an unbalanced set of cases would also have been limited, as the dependent variable (the evolution of collaboration in strategic alliances) would have largely been an artifact of the selection criteria (i.e. the presence or absence of initial conditions versus learning processes). Despite this carefully crafted approach to theoretical sampling, the author acknowledges that the sampling might have affected the empirical results. As he notes in the limitations section,

> The choice of cases, in retrospect, probably affects the research findings. We controlled for the potential value of the opportunities our sample firms were

> pursuing – i.e., all our projects were aimed at opportunities where a market existed – and for the technologies and competencies of the partners – i.e., all the partnerships studied brought together the required technologies and competencies to address the opportunity successfully. (Doz, 1996: p. 80)

At the same time, he also quickly dismissed his own self-criticism by emphasizing that the decisive factor in the research design was not the presence or absence of initial conditions versus learning outcomes, but the partners' skills in putting them together over the course of the alliance: "The economic value of the alliance was potentially there. The issue was whether the partners could combine their resources successfully, not whether they had them or not" (Doz, 1996: p. 80).

What about the dependent variable, that is, the collaboration of cooperation in strategic alliances? Recall that, in case studies, the selection on the dependent variable represents a form of sampling bias, especially if cases are selected from only one end of the covariational spectrum. In short, for reducing bias, we need both successful and unsuccessful cases which lie across a range of variance. And that is exactly what characterized the sample in Doz's study. As Doz points out in his section on theory building and testing: "Whereas the Ciba Geigy–Alza partnership was seen, by its participants, as having had mixed results, the others were seen, in retrospect, as a failure (AT&T–Olivetti) and a success (GE–SNECMA). We selected these two cases expecting maximum differences in processes, testing the robustness of our framework" (Doz, 1996: p. 59).

7.3.4.3 Controls

An essential ingredient in the case study design is that we compare cases that are similar with regard to conditions that are not part of the theoretical predictions and dissimilar with regard to the dependent and independent variables. Flatly put, we are trying to compare apples with apples, not apples with oranges. What we see in Doz's case is a selection of partnerships in three different industry contexts (pharmaceutical, office electronics, and jet engines). The first thing that comes to mind here is the question, what did all these different alliances have in common? That is, to what extent were they comparable? Keeping the industry context constant was not one of Doz's main preoccupations. Or maybe it was simply difficult to find the "right" cases (i.e. those that exhibit the characteristics described in Section 7.3.4.2 and in particular with regard to a minimum of co-variance between dependent and independent variables). Doz flatly admitted that "While access considerations did not allow to hold the industry external environment meaningfully constant, the individual projects studied all involved the combination of skills between the partners to pursue a new opportunity subject to significant market and technical uncertainties which could only be resolved over time rather than at the inception of the relationship" (Doz, 1996: p. 57). So, at first sight, Doz (1996) would appear to have compared apples and pears (and even pineapples), as the cases came from three different industry contexts. Are we right? Well, not really, since the common denominator on the case level (more on level of analysis in just a second) was that all the cases involved skill combinations needed to pursue a new market opportunity. All the cases had issues which could only be resolved over time, and not at the beginning of the relationship (thus providing the balanced conditions between the two independent variables as discussed in Section 7.3.4.2). In fact, the multitude of industrial contexts on the case level allowed Doz to claim greater generalizability (i.e. greater external validity and applicability across different industry contexts). Despite this, the author humbly chose to not underscore this benefit.

7.3.4.4 *Cases, Embedded Units, and Level of Analysis*

Technically speaking, Doz used an overall multiple embedded design, since there were several projects investigated within each alliance. We are saying "overall" here, as the sophistication of the design only becomes apparent if we examine "how" he sequentially analyzed the three alliances (i.e. the three "cases") and how the research question(s) and empirical foci evolved during the course of the sequencing. In other words, how the initial design (based on the first case, Ciba Geigy–Alza) was extended and even replicated in the remaining two cases (AT&T–Olivetti, GE–SNECMA) is what makes the design sophisticated. But before we get there, some thoughts on the cases and the level of analysis are in order.

As we have discussed in Chapters 5 and 6, a main benefit of (any) embedded design is that it automatically controls for several contextual variables within the case in which the embedded units are being studied. By definition, if we study two projects in one alliance involving the same partners, we ensure that there are no alternative explanations coming in (which might have happened if we study similar projects in different alliances involving different partners). Doz was very clear about this design right at the start of his paper's methodology section:

> A nested approach to individual cases was used, by selecting two projects within each of three multipoint alliances. This allowed us to distinguish

> between project-level, alliance-level, and corporate-level data and analysis. Each case study thus focused on one particular product area, and on one product partnership within that area, two such product partnerships being researched in each alliance. (Doz, 1996: p. 57)

The benefit of this approach was outlined two pages later in the paper, where Doz was not shy to circumscribe the benefits of controlling for corporate and geographic contexts for internal validity. In fact, as the following quote illustrates eloquently, not all projects even within the same alliance were considered equally successful. Thus, there was a degree of variance in the dependent variable, corresponding to nonequivalent values on the independent variable, even on the level of the embedded units (in addition to the case level). Note that, in the following quote, Doz never directly mentioned the benefits for internal validity but instead "walked the talk" (Gibbert & Ruigrok, 2010), that is, he transparently relayed the benefits of the sampling decisions on various levels of analysis.

> The three cases offered the additional benefit of being multipoint partner-ships, involving different technologies and products, allowing comparison of process variable differences between the "cases within the case" while holding overall corporate and geographic contexts constant. The fact that some of the individual projects, within the same alliance, were significantly more suc-cessful than others allowed significant analysis of project-level conditions, as distinct from partnership or corporate-level conditions. (Doz, 1996: p. 59)

What we see in Doz's case is the most complex of designs, that is, a multiple embedded design. Since this is a multiple embedded case study design, the main level of analysis is the case level, which are the three alliances. Despite this, a significant amount of theory-building happens on the project level, which represents another level of analysis present in each of the cases. As such the projects are the embedded units. In fact, toward the end of the paper, Doz summarized the performance differences of the individual projects within each alliance as follows: "The research reported here draws on a very small purposive sample, with an inductive model drawn from one case (including two contrasted projects, one successful, one unsuccessful), replicated and elaborated on two other alliances (another four projects), one successful, one unsuccessful" (Doz, 1996: p. 79).

7.3.5   Sequencing Case Study Designs

What makes this study a landmark, then (quite apart from emerging as the single-most rigorous paper in a sample of all case studies over 20 years, see

Gibbert et al., 2008)? What is remarkable is that the author chose to relay the various cases individually, that is, as a series of individual studies. Recall that the first study was Ciba Geigy–Alza, which was used to generate a (tentative theoretical framework). The results were "mixed" in the sense that the mediating role of learning processes could not be fully separated from the impact of initial conditions. Despite this, this first case yielded that very insight in the first place (however tentative it might have been at the time).

The second case (AT&T Olivetti) was considered a failure. Why a failure, and how did studying a failure and studying it as a second step in theory building provide consequential insights? As Doz explained:

> The AT&T–Olivetti relationship, which suffered from many of the same issues as the alliance between CG and AZ, allows us to consider more clearly a source of difficulty which also surfaced between AZ and CG: a difference in issue identification and decision-making speed between the partners. Olivetti (OL) would come with very quick, incremental suggestions to "improve" the relationship, based on issues OL's management had identified, worked on and "resolved" quickly. AT&T, a bigger, slower, more bureaucratic organization, would not be able to follow OL's speed in neither issue identification nor decision making. As a result, very seldom were the two partners able to jointly consider the same issue in the same time frame. (Doz, 1996: p. 70)

Then the third case put the spotlight on an even more extreme case of initial conditions. Doz managed to reveal the causalities that were apparent (albeit to a lesser degree) in the first case in more graphic detail. In the words of the author, it was worth perusing the ensuing theory-building:

> A first step in building an alliance evolution framework, and in answering our initial research question, is therefore to recognize that initial conditions may determine alliance outcomes when these conditions are highly inertial, i.e. when they lock partners into a repeated mode of interaction, with little learning of each interaction, with typically greater frustration on the part of the partners, both about their interactions, and the lack of progress of their alliances. (Doz, 1996: 70)

The third case (GE SNECMA) was a success. What does that mean? With regard to the relationship between initial conditions and learning processes, we would expect initial conditions that were conducive to learning processes to be indicators of enduring alliance success. And this is exactly what the third case illustrated:

> Conversely, initial conditions that foster learning, on the part of the partners, about the environment of their relationship, the task at hand,

each other and how to work together, their respective skills, and their motives, trigger an evolutionary path for the alliance: as learning takes place, the partners take that learning on board, and move away from the initial conditions to establish new conditions in light of the lessons drawn from that learning. (Doz, 1996: 70)

Note that the three cases also featured embedded units, with individual projects being more or less successful, thus replicating the findings on the case level. As we discussed in Section 7.3.4.4 and in this section, the inclusion of such embedded designs (focusing on projects within the overall alliance) within the sequence of three alliances afforded maximum control of context and therefore curbed alternative explanations. Each case/alliance as such constituted a kind of field experiment in which successful and unsuccessful projects replicated the results on the case level. This is a significant step up in terms of ensuring the causality and veracity of the findings, as theoretical replication was performed on the unit level where, by definition, the industry, company, and other contextual variables were constant. The research design provided internal validity on more levels than one.

Was the study designed this way from the start? In other words, did the author report the insights chronologically? The paper would appear to suggest that he did, although it is not 100 percent transparent with regard to the actual sequence in which these cases were studied. Alza and Ciba Geigy were studied between 1977 and 1982, AT&T and Olivetti between 1983 and 1989, and GE–SNECMA starting in the 1960s and continuing even while the paper was published (Doz, 1996: p. 57). Thus, while it seems abundantly clear that the first two cases must have been studied in the sequence in which they were reported in the final article (see also tables 1 and 2 in the Doz paper, which clearly provide the timeframe for the first and second case including the sub-projects), it is unclear whether the one successful case was indeed explored last (we noted that a table including timeline for the "last" case is absent in the paper).

7.4 How to Report Sequencing Case Study Designs?

Does it matter whether the sequence of the studies as reported in the final write-up corresponds to the sequence in which they were actually studied? Remember our earlier discussion (see the box titles "But someone ALSO asked me . . . . . . is sequencing case study design an iterative process?") on the iterative cycles in qualitative research and how it can inform our own sequencing of case study design. While these iterative cycles of theoretical refinement are seen as the cornerstone of theoretical rigor for case study research, they are rarely reported. For example, a recent review found that the transparency with which authors relay just how this iterative sensemaking evolved represents one of the least-featured methodological traits in published grounded theory research (Nair & Gibbert, 2016). What do we learn from this? It would appear that a key criterion for rigor in qualitative field research is the transparency with which the iterative cycles of data collection and analysis (and further data collection and analysis) are reported. However, this discussion should also extend to how the different case study designs were sequenced, and which aspect of the iterative cycle (i.e. which insight, or memo) eventually led to the subsequent case study designs in the sequence. The Doz (1996) case is a shining example for just that transparency, which not only gave a more complete picture of the reality of a strategic alliance formation–learning relationship but also provided fine-grained evidence of the causalities between the individual constructs. Furthermore, this led to greater replicability (read: reliability) of the research findings. We prefer to call this the "genesis" of the research findings.

Therefore, our answer to the question on how to report sequencing is that researchers need to be transparent about the sequencing. Transparent reporting illustrates methodological sophistication to the benefit of the research community. Doz chose to report the "mixed results" of the first case, Ciba Geigy–Alza, for instance. What if Doz chose not to report these findings? Well, this would have resulted in a file-drawer problem (Rosenthal, 1979). In that case, any future researcher who might want to investigate an effect thinking it is *new* would not have been aware that Doz already investigated it. If Ciba Geigy–Alza case findings were locked up and hidden away in some file drawer, future researchers might have engaged in futile efforts trying to investigate something that has already been investigated.

Thus, what really matters is transparently relaying the sequencing of your case study designs, and the insights and rationale that prompted this sequencing. In the case of Doz (1996), the sequence of the different cases in the Doz paper produced a cogent narrative where we first have mixed results (Ciba Geigy–Alza), which led to a tentative framework produced in an inductive fashion. The very fact that this study produced "mixed" results is intriguing as it opened the floor to the subsequent two cases. However, in Doz (1996) it was not clear whether the two subsequent cases were investigated simultaneously or separately. This is perhaps our only qualm with this paper, because for transparency's sake the sequence in which these case study designs were undertaken and the rationale that prompted subsequent designs should have been reported. Indeed, even if the narration of a paper follows a different sequence, we would still urge researchers to be transparent about the sequencing, for instance in the appendix of the paper. Despite this minor hiccup, Doz's paper is a stellar example of how you can engage with sequencing case study designs. This is because, after the "mixed results" from the first case, it was followed by a failed case (AT&T–Olivetti); and then, as the icing on the cake, it was followed by a successful case (General Electric–NECMA) that followed the same theoretical predictions. Thus, the narrative started with mixed results to develop a tentative framework inductively which was then "tested" deductively via a failed and a successful case, respectively, leading to a picture-perfect example of comparing polar opposites of failure and success (in that order) of a theoretical prediction. As such, what the Doz (1996) paper clearly highlighted is that the researcher did not shy away from being imaginatively curious, by using different combinations of case study designs and logical reasoning to reach his end goal of providing a comprehensive understanding of the phenomenon. And indeed, it was his willingness to sequence case study designs that allowed him to make a powerful and novel contribution in his field!

REFERENCES

Bloor, M. & Wood, F. (2006). Theoretical saturation. In *Keywords in Qualitative Methods*. Sage Research Methods. Available at: https://www.doi.org/10.4135/9781849209403 (last accessed May 24, 2022).

Corbin, J. & Strauss, A. (2014). *Basics of Qualitative Research: Techniques and Procedures for Developing Grounded Theory*. Thousand Oaks: Sage.

Doz, Y. L. (1996). The evolution of cooperation in strategic alliances: Initial conditions or learning processes? *Strategic Management Journal*, 17(S1), 55–83.

Gibbert, M., & Ruigrok, W. (2010). The "what" and "how" of case study rigor: Three strategies based on published work. *Organizational Research Methods*, 13(4), 710–737.

Gibbert, M., Ruigrok, W. & Wicki, B. (2008). What passes as a rigorous case study? *Strategic Management Journal*, 29(13), 1465–1474.

Lack, D. (1983). *Darwin's Finches*. New York: Cambridge University Press.

Magnani, G. & Zucchella, A. (2019). Coping with uncertainty in the internationalisation strategy: An exploratory study on entrepreneurial firms. *International Marketing Review*, 36(1), 131–163.

Meijer, H. (2018, July 30). Origin of the species: where did Darwin's finches come from? *The Guardian*. Available at: www.theguardian.com/science/

2018/jul/30/origin-of-the-species-where-did-darwins-finches-come-from (last accessed July 27, 2022).

Mills, A. J., Durepos, G. & Wiebe, E. (2010, December 27). Iterative. *Sage Research Methods*. Available at: https://methods.sagepub.com/reference/encyc-of-case-study-research/n185.xml (last accessed July 27, 2022).

Nair, L. B. & Gibbert, M. (2016). Hot on the audit trail: How to assess methodological transparency of grounded theory in management? In *Academy of Management Proceedings*. New York: Academy of Management, 13758.

Nicholls, H. (2017). Evolution: Darwin's domestic discoveries. *Nature*, 548, 389–390.

Podos, J. (2001). Correlated evolution of morphology and vocal signal structure in Darwin's finches. *Nature*, 409(6817), 185–188.

Ritchie, J., Lewis, J., Nicholls, C. M., & Ormston, R. (2013). *Qualitative Research Practice: A Guide for Social Science Students and Researchers*. Thousand Oaks: Sage.

Rosenthal, R. (1979). The file drawer problem and tolerance for null results. *Psychological Bulletin*, 86(3), 638–641.

Sulloway, F. J. (2005, December). The evolution of Charles Darwin. Natural History Museum. *Smithsonian Magazine*. Available at: www.smithsonianmag.com/science-nature/the-evolution-of-charles-darwin-110234034/ (last accessed December 13, 2021).

CHAPTER 8

More on Sequencing Case Study Designs
Deductive–Inductive

8.1 Discovering a "Black Swan" and Diving into Deductive–Inductive Sequencing Case Study Designs

In the last chapter, we introduced you to our take on what it means to be imaginatively curious, and how leveraging the strengths of different case study designs (i.e. sequencing case study designs) can help satiate said curiosity. In this chapter, we still continue with our journey on explaining the many different ways you can sequence case study designs by introducing the deductive–inductive mode of sequencing. Through Chapters 7 and 8, we hope to inspire you to use your imaginative curiosity to design your very own sequenced designs.

To continue this journey on sequencing, we take inspiration from our black swan example discussed in Chapter 3. Let's imagine that you are an explorer. You have seen swans throughout your adult life. Given the many swans that you have seen, you have conjectured that "all swans are white." Therefore, if as an explorer you end up on the southwest shores of Australia for the first time, and you end up bumping into a black swan for the first time, this would surely intrigue your imaginative curiosity. Given this "unexpected" new observation, what do you conjecture now? In all likeliness, you will speculate that not all swans are white.

BUT BEFORE WE MOVE ON LET'S THINK ABOUT THE ...

... DESIGN DECISIONS ON THE "BLACK SWAN" EXAMPLE BEING DISCUSSED
By referring to Figure 7.1, consider the following questions when you spot a "black swan":

Q.1   Which logical reasoning are you using (i.e. inductive, deductive, or abductive)? Justify.
Q.2   Which case study design are you using? (i.e. single holistic, single embedded, multiple holistic, or multiple embedded). Justify.
Q.3   After deciding your case study design, indicate what is the case (or cases) and the embedded units (if they are present). Justify.

As an explorer–researcher, you are engaging in deductive reasoning as you are disconfirming the statement that "all swans are white." So, what kind of case study design are you using? Assuming that you only saw one "black swan," you are using a single holistic design. But do you think you should stop here? After all, this is the very first "black swan" that you have seen. So, wouldn't you be intrigued to move beyond the mere understanding now that "not all swans are white"? In such a situation, which arises often in the research process, wouldn't you like to remain imaginatively curious by following up on this interesting insight?

BUT BEFORE WE MOVE ON LET'S BE IMAGINATIVELY CURIOUS ...

... BY SEQUENCING THE NEXT CASE STUDY DESIGN
Look at Figure 8.1. Your first case study design is a single holistic design that follows a deductive reasoning. Now think of the second case study design that you can sequence by sharing the design decisions you will take. Justify your design decisions.

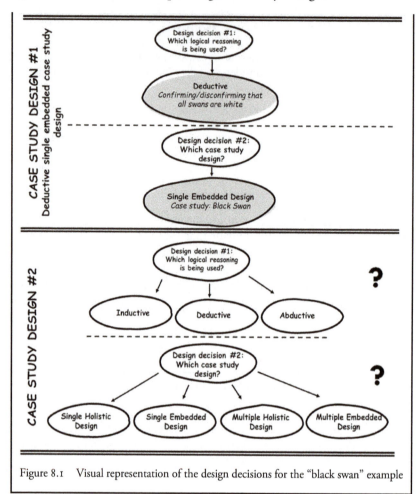

Figure 8.1   Visual representation of the design decisions for the "black swan" example

A case study design that can possibly be sequenced after this deductive single holistic design would be one that follows an inductive logical reasoning. After all, this is your first ever sighting of a "black swan." You might like to know more about this "new" type of swan by generating explanations on why the swan is black on the southwest shores of Australia. Moreover, you might suspect that the black swan you saw isn't the only black swan in Australia. As such, as a curious researcher, you would be interested in finding more black swans to generate new explanations regarding their blackness and special properties. If we consider "black swan" as your case; and you sequence your next case study design by studying more than one black swan, then you are using a multiple holistic case study design. So, you will be sequencing your deductive single holistic case study design with an inductive multiple holistic case study design.

Let us discuss another example, but this time from the field of political science. For this we take inspiration from an earlier example discussed in Chapter 4 from Robinson and Acemoglu's (2012) book, "Why Nations Fail: The Origins of Power, Prosperity, and Poverty." Let's imagine that as a political scientist you are interested in understanding the causes of inequality. You come across the well-accepted "culture hypothesis" which states that much of the world inequality stems from the "culture" of that region, namely the religion, national ethics, social norms, and values. But as a political scientist, very much like Robinson and Acemoglu, you can dispute this claim by bringing regions or cities that share the same culture yet have differences in the level of inequalities. One example could be a comparison between South Korea and North Korea, both of which lie in the Korean peninsula and are culturally similar yet have different levels of inherent inequalities. Let's reflect on what kind of case study design this comparison would entail. What is the logical reasoning at play here? Given that you are disconfirming (or confirming) the "culture hypothesis," you are undertaking deductive reasoning here. Now let's think of your second design decision – what is your case study design? If you treat the Korean peninsula as your case, then you are undertaking a single embedded design where your case is the Korean peninsula (i.e. the case you want to theorize), and your embedded units are the two countries, namely South and North Korea.

Perhaps you already know what we want to say here, that is, we should not stop here! Ask yourself – Why are there different levels of inequalities in the Korean peninsula given the cultural similarities? You can address this question by sequencing another case study design to the single embedded design of the Korean peninsula and the two embedded units (i.e. South and North Korea). You have to go inductive here! And if you are like Robinson and Acemoglu (2012), you would have induced that inequalities originate due to the type of "institutions" present within the different countries of the Korean peninsula. That is, while South Korea has "inclusive institutions" that benefit the masses, North Korea has "extractive institutions" (i.e. the opposite of inclusive institutions) that do not work for the masses.

You can then of course follow it up with yet another case study design, where you take on a deductive approach for confirming/disconfirming your inductively generated insights from the second design. For instance, you can compare two cities that share the same culture – Nogales (Arizona) and

Nogales (Sonora). Indeed, what you would find is that both cities, while sharing the same culture, have different levels of inequalities due to different institutions. Nogales (Arizona) has inclusive institutions, whereas Nogales (Sonora) has extractive institutions. These insights will help you confirm your theoretical insights from the earlier, inductive case study design.

BUT BEFORE WE MOVE ON LET'S BE IMAGINATIVELY CURIOUS ...

... BY IDENTIFYING WHAT KIND OF CASE STUDY DESIGN YOU ARE UNDERTAKING
FOR NOGALES (ARIZONA) AND NOGALES (SONORA)

Q.1   Which logical reasoning are you using (i.e. inductive, deductive, or abductive)? Justify.
Q.2   Which case study design are you using? (i.e. single holistic, single embedded, multiple holistic, or multiple embedded). Justify.

So, coming back to the kind of case study design you are using, you need to first think about the kind of logical reasoning you are applying. Given that you are confirming/disconfirming your theoretical insights generated from the Korean peninsula, we would say you are being deductive here. Now regarding your case study design, it all boils down to what your cases and level of analysis are. If your level of analysis are the cities, then this makes Nogales (Arizona) and Nogales (Sonora) your cases, thus landing you in a multiple holistic case study design. We provide a visual representation on the sequencing of case study designs in Figure 8.2.

8.2   Deductive–Inductive Sequencing: Are Outliers Nuisances or Opportunities?

In Chapter 7, we saw an example of a sequence of case study designs, which started with an inductive approach which resulted in a conceptual model. The model was subsequently tested in a deductive co-variational approach, which included both successful and unsuccessful cases. In other words, extreme cases were compared along a spectrum of possible outcomes. Note that this covariational approach in the second and third case was feasible only after the analysis of the first case, which provided the independent and dependent variables in the first place. On a different note, in this chapter we have briefly introduced you to scenarios in which a different kind of logical reasoning for sequencing case study designs, namely deductive–

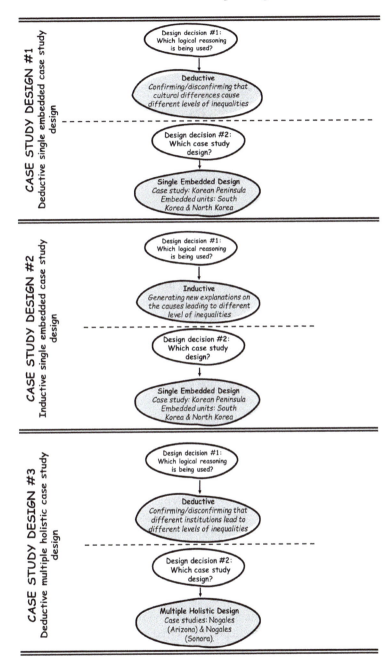

Figure 8.2 Visual representation of the design decisions for theorizing inequalities

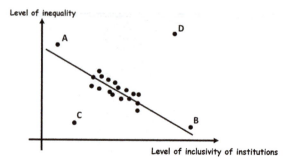

Figure 8.3   Graphical representation of model fit outliers and prediction outliers
(deviant cases)

inductive reasoning, is leveraged. In this section, we will explore another type of deductive–inductive sequencing that can be undertaken.

For this purpose, we will explore the study by Zott and Huy (2007) in-depth. The authors here were interested in investigating the link between impression management and resource acquisition by start-up companies. An initial set of 26 cases was identified, but analysis then focused only on seven extreme cases. Of these seven, there were several that did not fit the theoretical predictions. Therefore, as we will see in the rest of this chapter, beyond an inductive–deductive sequence, we can also engage in a deductive–inductive sequence by examining the cases that do *not* fit the theoretical model. To understand the dynamics behind this logic, a short foray into outliers is in order before we dive more deeply into the Zott and Huy (2007) paper.

8.2.1   A Tale of Two Outliers

In qualitative case study research, a researcher can compare extreme cases or "polar opposites" in a covariational manner or theoretical replication mode (e.g. Eisenhardt, 1989) for theory enhancement. Such an analysis can even focus exclusively on the so-called model fit outliers. But what are model fit outliers? Let us refer to our example in Section 8.1 on theorizing inequalities by sequencing case study designs. As you might remember, the research identified that higher levels of inclusive institutions lead to lower levels of inequalities. For explanation sake, let us represent this using a (hypothetical) graph, in which the horizontal x-axis represents "level of inclusivity of institutions" (i.e. the independent variable) and the vertical y-axis represents "levels of inequality" (i.e. the dependent variable) (see Figure 8.3).

The solid line (also known as the regression line in the quantitative world) simply shows that a higher level of inclusive institutions leads to lower levels of inequalities. Each point on the graph represents a country. So, what are model fit outliers here? These are the points on the graph that represent extremely high/low values on independent variable(s) and, correspondingly, on the dependent variable(s). In Figure 8.3, these would be points A and B. You might be wondering what the value in studying these "model fit outliers" (namely points A and B) are. There is indeed value, primarily because the causal dynamics in these outliers are transparently observable (Eisenhardt, 1989). Time and resource constraints will not allow for a qualitative exploration of all the points in our hypothetical graph. However, the perusal of model fit outliers might reveal the causal relationships and processes underway in this larger body of observations more crisply and with less resources.

Consequently, model fit outliers positively influence the fit of the model (Aguinis et al., 2013: p. 275). This simply means that these outliers are "on" the regression line but are outlying in that they assume relatively (i.e. relative to the main body of observations) high/low values on the independent factor(s) (as evident from points A and B in Figure 8.3). As such, comparing polar opposites or model fit outliers is the essence of the "deductive" step in a sequence of case study designs. At the same time, precisely because it is deductive, its focus is on theory testing. Therefore, these outliers are likely to offer only limited theory building potential. The reason for this is because the model fit outliers align with the other cases (e.g. the less extreme ones) illustrating the relationships between focal variables (i.e. independent and dependent variables). Thus, analysis of model fit outliers is unlikely to provide insights that go beyond what a theory based on the less extreme (i.e. average) cases would generally predict. Instead, they are best used for theory testing, as we have seen in the case of the Doz (1996) study discussed in Chapter 7. Doz (1996) used the polar opposites or model fit outliers in the second and third case study precisely to have a conclusive test of the theoretical model, which was inductively developed in the first case study.

Can we also reverse this logic of sequencing research designs such that the sequence is deductive–inductive? In other words, can we start by focusing on a (larger) body of observations, pick out the extreme cases, analyze them, and find novel insights? Can we thus move from the general to the particular, from the average to the uncommon? The answer is yes, and we will try to showcase this, again using an exemplar from our previous research (i.e. Gibbert et al., 2021) which focused on a different kind of outlier, namely "prediction outliers." So, what are prediction outliers? And how do they differ from model fit outliers? Prediction outliers, similar to model fit outliers, have extreme values on the focal variables (i.e. independent and dependent variables). But, unlike model fit outliers, prediction outliers are characterized by large model residuals (only) – that simply means that, unlike pure model fit outliers, prediction outliers are characterized by model mis-fit and are "off" the regression line. They are typically referred to as "deviant cases," precisely because they deviate from theoretical expectations (and from now on we use the term "deviant case" more frequently to denote "prediction outliers") (Gibbert et al., 2021). The model misfit of the deviant cases opens new avenues for investigating alternative explanations, which is why they should not be ignored as irrelevant oddities. Instead, we should go after them deliberately to explore possibilities off the beaten theoretical tracks. In Figure 8.3 these prediction outliers are represented by points C and D.

Ignoring deviant cases is particularly problematic from a theory-building perspective, since analysis of these cases may shed new light on systematic inconsistencies and emerging theory–data conflicts which occur whilst we try to reconcile theoretical predictions with real-world observations. For instance, if we go back to our anti-culture hypothesis example, a possible prediction outlier could be China, as it is a country with low levels of inequality, but it also has less inclusive institutions. An important point worth keeping in mind is deviant cases do not necessarily invalidate theories outright. However, they may reveal boundary conditions, contingencies, and conditional effects that had not been considered previously by the researcher. A quantitative study in criminology provides an interesting example. Giordano (1989) used the logic of deviant case analysis to identify youths who, based on the theorizing at the time, should have been delinquent but were not. Perusal of the outlying observations pointed to a so-far overlooked variable in causes of delinquency: The strength of ties with parents. This insight contributed to criminology by suggesting that even if all other factors point to delinquency, strong ties with parents might attenuate these factors, and ultimately curb delinquency. If similar deviant cases recur (as in fact they did in Giordano's study on youth delinquency), a researcher therefore may use such cases to establish (and possibly push) the boundary for the utility of the theory of interest (see also Sullivan 2011: pp. 907–908).

BUT BEFORE WE MOVE ON LET'S THINK ABOUT THE ...

　　... ZOTT AND HUY (2007) PAPER "HOW ENTREPRENEURS USE SYMBOLIC
　　　　MANAGEMENT TO ACQUIRE RESOURCES"
Read the Zott and Huy (2007) paper carefully, and answer the following
questions:

Q.1　What is the research question?
Q.2　What are the cases? How are these cases selected?
Q.3　Are there outliers present in the paper? If so, what kind of outliers
　　　(prediction or model fit outliers)?
Q.4　Are there any embedded units? If so, what are they?
Q.5　What are the independent, dependent, and control variables?
Q.6　What case study designs are being used? What are the different levels of
　　　analysis?
Q.7　Do you see any sequencing of case study designs? If so, what are they
　　　and in which order do they appear?

8.3　Zott and Huy (2007) As an Illustrative Example of Sequencing Case Study Designs: Deductive–Inductive

8.3.1　Components of the Case Study Design

8.3.1.1　Research Question
The article by Zott and Huy (2007) titled "How entrepreneurs use
symbolic management to acquire resources" was the only qualitative (top
management journal) article in 20 years which explored deviant cases in
detail (Gibbert et al., 2014). The authors of this article start off with the
observation that acquiring resources represents a key challenge for nascent
organizations. According to them, the young, inexperienced, and unpro-
ven organizations were particularly challenged since resource holders
were often reluctant to commit their resources to such new ventures.
The starting point for the qualitative study by Zott and Huy (2007) was
the lack of clarity regarding the specific actions which the entrepreneurs
engage in when acquiring resources. They were interested in understanding the theoretical rationale behind these actions: "In many instances,
researchers have tended to look at these actions as a kind of checklist but
have not really explored how and why performing them would have a
differential impact on resource acquisition" (Zott & Huy, 2007: p. 2).

Note that the research question changed over the course of the study, and the authors reveal these changes in the final article. This is important, as the article not only embraces the iterative cycles of qualitative research (as discussed in Chapter 7); but also allows us to trace the genesis of the theoretical contribution, and more importantly shows us that they, the authors, were not afraid to be imaginatively curious. To begin with, the authors started by being broadly informed by the literature on impression management. They were particularly interested in the type of actions entrepreneurs take to impress resource holders (i.e. venture capitalists) and to convince them to provide funds. "We began our research without formalizing any expectations of what actions entrepreneurs take to acquire resources. Formulating precise hypotheses seemed premature because current entrepreneurship theories are underdeveloped (Venkataraman, 1997)" (Zott & Huy, 2007: p. 74).

How the research question changed becomes apparent only in the data analysis section, where the authors recounted how the identified seven cases roughly followed the expected covariational pattern, that is, how high impression management led to high resource acquisition (recall what we said earlier on the idea of comparing model fit outliers). Despite this, there were several cases which did not follow this pattern, and high impression management in those cases was associated only with limited resource acquisition potential (these are the ones we call deviant cases). In other words, the general pattern among the selected model fit outliers was not satisfactory, as there were some (the authors do not disclose the number) ventures that did not "fit" the model and as such were deviant outliers. A closer look at these deviant cases revealed an important new insight, namely the fact that some of the entrepreneurs behind these deviant cases also appeared to use symbols to convey their business model. This insight subsequently led to the revised research question. In view of the absence/presence of symbolic action in these deviant cases, the authors went back to the main body of observations and re-analyzed the data from the perspective of symbolic action as a subset of impression management.

Now, let's take a step back from the evolution of the research question and consider what this means for the write-up of the article, especially when it comes to the front end (introduction and theoretical part) and the tail end (discussion). Given that there are roughly two different versions of the research question, which one should we pick to introduce the case study design, that is, which one is the "main" research question? Should the authors stick to a chronologically "authentic" approach and start with the first research question and then move on with the revised one? Let's see what this would mean for the front end. Basically, the entire theoretical framing would be on the vast body of literature on impression management in the context of resource acquisition. It would be fairly difficult to then argue that the study would be inductive, would it not? The alternative is to start with the second research question and focus straight on the (basically non-existent) literature on symbolic action in the context of resource acquisition. This approach would require an introduction that reverts the original sequence of the findings such that we argue that there is no literature investigating this phenomenon and, hence, the motivation for an inductive research design.

This is a clever move by the authors as it allowed them, in the tail end of the paper, to focus squarely on the second research question, illustrating how their findings enrich the literature by providing new types of actions that use symbols, together with the factors that make such symbolic actions more or less effective. The first sentence of the discussion kicks this off: "We motivated this study by asking what kinds of symbolic actions entrepreneurs use, how they use them, and why they could be effective for resource acquisition" (Zott & Huy, 2007: p. 96).

This move then provided the authors with a platform to dig deeper into the phenomenon, fleshing out its details in terms of the skillfulness and frequency of symbolic action, and any moderating factors that either attenuate these effects (such as structural similarity and intrinsic value of the venture) or increase them (such as uncertainty). Thus, they found that the higher the uncertainty, the more important the symbolic actions to acquire resources become. Likewise, the higher the structural similarity between the resource holder (in terms of the resource holders' and founders' norms, expectations, or status) and the venture, the less important the symbolic actions for bridging it become. Similarly, the higher the intrinsic value of the venture, the less important the symbolic action will be: "When entrepreneurs can point to impressive intrinsic track records and achievements, they do not have to rely on the symbolic dimension as much as if they have few such resources" (Zott & Huy, 2007: p. 95).

8.3.1.2 *Theoretical Sampling, Prediction Outliers, and Controls*
As we emphasized in Chapter 5, selection of a case(s) is important, as the inferential power rests quite literally upon the case(s) that the researcher selects. Zott and Huy (2007) indicated that they used theoretical sampling to select their relevant cases. Let us analyze their carefully crafted and extremely controlled sampling strategy in some detail here. To begin with,

the authors (both from the business school INSEAD at its Fontainebleau/ Paris campus at the time) prevailed upon the business school's alumni database for an initial sample of interesting ventures:

> We searched a business school's data base of alumni who had become involved in entrepreneurial ventures after they graduated. We identified 230 people, whom we contacted by e-mail to explain the purpose of our research. We asked for entrepreneurs who (1) had launched a company within the past 18 months or were planning to do so in the next six months, (2) had their headquarters in the Greater London area, and (3) were willing to participate in a research project that might involve a substantial time commitment. (Zott & Huy, 2007: p. 74)

The rationale for sampling early ventures was to avoid sampling on the dependent variable, that is, to avoid sampling established ventures that already experienced some success. The rationale for the greater London area was to minimize (i.e. control for) the effect of environmental factors including socio-political context, business climate, and available resources (Zott & Huy, 2007: p. 74). Focusing on the greater London area was pragmatic as well, due to a convenient train connection between Paris's Gare du Nord and London's St. Pancras. Note that the authors' theoretical sampling strategy being practically convenient also controlled for a variety of factors on the individual/personal level of the entrepreneurs/founders:

> Most founders had graduated from the same top-tier business school, had very high average GMAT test scores (around 700), had an average of five years' professional experience before enrolling in the Master of Business Administration (MBA) program, and could access the school's vast and high-powered alumni network. Our selection thus controlled for aspects of human capital such as educational background, analytical skill, and managerial experience, as well as aspects of social capital, all of which are usually sources of heterogeneity in entrepreneurial ventures. (Zott & Huy, 2007: p. 75)

Out of the 230 contacted entrepreneurs, 83 replied and eventually 26 were retained for study. The rest were eliminated for a (plausible) reason. The main center of operations of the eliminated entrepreneurs was not within the greater London area and hence they eventually dropped out because of a lack of time to participate or other related issues. Thus, the authors relied on the impression management literature to theoretically sample a subset of 26 cases with varying degrees of impression management. Analysis then focused on seven extreme cases that were characterized by particularly high or low levels of impression management. Impression management theory was then used to code the interview and archival data from both entrepreneurs and resource holders in an attempt to uncover how entrepreneurs acquire resources. This theory predicted that high impression management activity positively influenced resource acquisition potential. In the initial analysis, the authors "First tried a theory-elaboration approach, in which we analyzed a sample of ventures that displayed high and low levels of impression management actions, according to the taxonomy proposed ..." (Zott & Huy, 2007: p. 14).

However, the ensuing analysis revealed several cases where high impression management was unexpectedly associated with moderate-to-low success. In other words, the authors found several deviant cases. This in turn led to a reanalysis of the existing data, with a focus specifically on symbolic action (rather than impression management, Zott & Huy 2007: p. 77). Consider how the authors relayed the crucial moment of discovery at this stage:

> The general pattern suggested that high impression management activity may be positively associated with high resource acquisition, but we were not fully satisfied, because a few ventures with high impression management actions experienced moderate to low success, so the impression management findings were imprecise. This dissatisfaction led us to reanalyze our data in a second step and focus on symbolic action as a subset of impression management. (Zott & Huy 2007: p. 77)

The authors then clearly described how new theoretical categories were used in the reanalysis of the data, now focusing specifically on symbolic action. Zott and Huy (2007) thus identified deviant cases (which were initially confusing due to them confounding impression management with symbolic action management). Subsequently, the omitted variable (symbolic action) improved the authors' understanding of the phenomenon by generating a new theory of resource acquisition that established that high (versus low) symbolic actions were consistently associated with high (versus low) resource acquisition. Note that the authors also went back to confirm this emergent theory with the original sample of 26 cases. Thus, they established the phenomenon not only in the deviant cases but also in the remaining typical cases, including those that appeared to follow the initially expected theoretical pattern. In particular, the authors emphasized that: "We could not find a single case among the 26 venture projects in which a low level of symbolic actions correlated with a high level of success in consistently attracting resources, nor could we find a case in which a high level of symbolic actions correlated with a low level of success" (Zott & Huy, 2007: p. 76).

Thus, rather than sweeping the "untidy" results of the first coding under the proverbial carpet of model-fit, the authors instead doggedly decided to follow up on those cases that did not fit the original assumptions (i.e. the deviant cases). Thereafter, they verified the emerging insights by checking with the empirical evidence of the remaining cases in the sample. A dedicated redesigning followed, which uncovered the theoretically consequential and hitherto overlooked variable in resource acquisition, which in turn became the key feature of the final article's story line, as we discussed in Section 8.3.1.1.

Ultimately, this approach enabled the authors to contribute to organization theory by demonstrating how variance in symbolic action management led to different resource acquisition outcomes, thereby generating a new theory that is both causally stronger (by introducing a so-far neglected variable), as well more generally applicable (the results were found to be replicable across all cases in the sample, with no more deviant cases in evidence), overall explaining a larger degree of variance. Put differently, the deviant cases provided the impetus to consider alternative explanations, thus providing a better understanding of the phenomenon with the existing data. In fact, the new focus on symbolic actions enabled the authors to nuance its impact even further by pointing to several moderating factors (e.g. structural similarity between resource holder and seeker, intrinsic quality of the venture, uncertainty in the marketplace, etc. (see Zott & Huy, 2007: pp. 36–39).

Highlighting the consequentiality of symbolic action as a key lever in resource acquisition represents a novel contribution to organization and entrepreneurship theory. In particular, prior theorizing on symbolic action had focused on how communication in response to an established organization's image affects its later performance, as well as how symbolic action and communication affect power and control relationships within firms. Unknown so far were the effects of symbolic action in resource acquisition strategies by new ventures. By disentangling them from impression management, the authors "hope(d) to restore the full richness of symbolic actions in organization studies" (Zott & Huy, 2007: p. 45).

8.3.1.3   Cases and Level of Analysis

It is clear that the cases in the Zott and Huy (2007) study were the individual ventures. Therefore, the level of analysis here was at the venture level. The data collection focused mainly on the founder so as to obtain data at the level of the venture. Data collection focused on interviews with two and three founders per venture. Furthermore, since what might appear to be a symbol to the entrepreneur might not come across as a symbol to the resource holder; the authors mentioned how they

> ... also interviewed important stakeholders, including co-founders, investors, employees, suppliers, customers, and board members. Some of the questions that we asked stakeholders other than co-founders included

"What resources did you provide to the venture, and why?" "Can you give us some examples of how the entrepreneurs approached and interacted with you?" and "What did you like, or like less, about the way the entrepreneur approached you and dealt with you?" (Zott & Huy, 2007: p. 76)

Overall, the authors coded an action as symbolic if it met at least one of the following conditions: "(1) it was clearly intended by the entrepreneur as a symbolic action, in that the actor displayed or tried to draw other people's attention to a meaning that went beyond its intrinsic content or functional use; (2) it was perceived as symbolic by the resource holder; or (3) we saw it as symbolic" (Zott & Huy, 2007: p. 77).

8.3.2 Sequencing Case Study Design and Additional Data Collection

Note that the sequence of research designs as found in Zott and Huy (2007) started deductively (by mapping the covariance of impression management and resource acquisition) and proceeded in an inductive manner (by focusing on the new variable "symbolic action" and then reanalyzing the existing data). When case study designs are sequenced, theory development cannot be fully realized without further data collection and analysis. In fact, it is this further data collection and analysis (as already discussed in Chapter 7) that can also help in designing a follow-up case study design to better address the needs of the research in hand (a.k.a sequencing case study design). In this sense, the deviant cases in Zott and Huy's (2007) dataset represent the starting point of, and momentum behind, an additional cycle of iterative theorizing which helped them to sequence their case study designs.

Let us make a sweeping statement regarding the choreography of inductive reasoning followed by Zott and Huy. If we start our case study with a deductive approach and if and when we find a deviant case, the researcher might consider going back to the study's original theoretical propositions and rechecking the causalities underlying the theory in the light of the said deviant cases. In a second step (i.e. the first in the subsequent cycle of iterative theorizing), the researcher could reason inductively and potentially also sample, collect, and analyze additional cases accordingly. All of these changes can be accommodated by sequencing the initial case study design with a new one. Ultimately, the cogency of the research results depends directly on how compelling the claim about the relationship between the observed dependent variables and the independent variables of interest is. The researcher should therefore aim to prove that the relationship is indeed caused by the variables of interest, rather than some other potentially plausible (but omitted) factors. In this context, Yin admonished his readers that "Without such redesign you risk being accused of distorting or ignoring the discovery, just to accommodate the original design. This condition leads quickly to a further accusation: that you have been selective in reporting your data to suit your preconceived ideas" (Yin 2003: p. 51).

Redesigning may involve theoretical sampling of additional cases for the purpose of replicating or complementing the deviant case, as well as making changes in the case study data collection protocol more generally, in particular with regard to control variables that could influence the results. And this sequencing of case study designs precisely happened in the study by Zott and Huy (2007), where the unexpected discovery that the theoretically sampled cases actually did not support the initial expectation (i.e. high impression management leads to high resource acquisition potential) led to a reanalysis of the data, with a focus specifically on symbolic action (Zott & Huy, 2007).

8.4   More on Deductive–Inductive Sequencing of Case Study Designs: Deviant Cases, Omitted Variable Bias, and Internal Validity

Ultimately, the cogency of the research results in a deductive–inductive sequence depends directly on how compelling the claim is that observed outcomes (i.e. dependent variables) are caused by the independent variables of interest, rather than other potentially plausible (but omitted) factors. Cook and Campbell (1979) have coined the widely accepted term of "internal validity" to refer to such covariational relationships between independent variable(s) and dependent variable(s). Cases should therefore exhibit strong differences with respect to the main independent variables and corresponding (theoretically motivated) differences on the dependent variable(s) and be otherwise as similar as possible (i.e. on your control variables).

Typically, there is "something special" (King et al. 1994: p. 203) about deviant cases if and when they occur. A deviant case may hold the clue to confounding variable(s) (i.e. a variable that is affecting both the dependent and independent variable) which, if included in the conceptual framework, will influence the results. Because internal validity refers to the causal relationships between variables and results. Explicitly following up on – and including into the research design – any additional variables of interest that a deviant case(s) suggests, constitutes a key strategy for enhancing a theory's internal validity. Alternatively, deviant cases, when more fully explored, may lead to entirely different theories that complement or compete with existing, prior theories. When cases are chosen to represent a range of variation between variables of interest, the relationship between the variables of interest becomes more plausible, its underlying causality becomes stronger, and consequently its internal validity becomes greater. Thus, explicitly including deviant cases in the analysis (rather than ignoring them) may yield a richer, more plausible, and ultimately more internally valid theory.

In short, the deductive–inductive sequencing of case study design provides a widely applicable approach to perform just this kind of constructive in-depth outlier analysis for the benefit of internal validity of the (new) theory. If transparently performed, theory building from deviant cases therefore constitutes a kind of gold standard for rigorous theoretical contributions (i.e. contributions that go beyond mainstream conceptual development).

8.5   Reporting the Sequencing of Case Study Designs

As showcased in this chapter and in Chapter 7, the sequencing of case study designs can be undertaken in pluralistic ways. Sequencing adds great value to the theorizing process as it leads the researchers to engage with their imaginative curiosity by providing a better theoretical understanding of the phenomenon. The deductive–inductive sequence represents one of the many ways in which you can engage with sequencing case study designs. But such "pluralism" can only thrive if we transparently report the sensemaking procedures involved in the research process. For instance, comparisons with existing theory and other cases which confirms and disconfirms the initial findings of a study, should be transparently reported. As discussed in the previous chapters, more specifically in Chapter 7, case study researchers are required to go back and forth between existing theoretical preconceptions and actual emerging findings through iterative data collection and data analysis.

Therefore, to researchers interested in conducting case study research which follows a deductive–inductive sequence relying on deviant cases, we would recommend a transparent reporting of the detection of said deviant cases, as Zott and Huy (2007) did. While researchers might have valid reasons for not analyzing outliers in some studies, reporting their occurrence transparently will still trigger theoretical contributions by offering other interested researchers the possibility to explore them and subsequently make theoretical contributions.

The deductive–inductive method and its focus on deviant cases represent a productive method for enhancing our understanding of existing theories and may hold the potential to point to additional and, so far, neglected variables that might be consequential for theorizing. Analyzing deviant cases heads-on represents a sophisticated theorizing process. Methodologically, it picks up the additional variables and manifests how they behave along a range of possible dependent variables, thereby going beyond testing the boundary conditions of an established theory and actually moving towards advancing extant theory (impression management, as in the case of Zott and Huy's study) or building a new theory (on symbolic actions).

Milan Kundera, in "The Art of the Novel" defined "idyll" as "the condition of the world before the first conflict, or beyond conflicts, or with conflicts that are misunderstandings, thus false conflicts" (Kundera, 1989: p. 121). What we can learn from the article by Zott and Huy (2007) is that we should not be shy to abstain from "idyllic" write-ups and must instead transparently report on conflicts between empirical findings and theoretical predictions to better understand the phenomenon that we are researching.

REFERENCES

Aguinis, H., Gottfredson, R. K., & Joo, H. (2013). Best-practice recommendations for defining, identifying, and handling outliers. *Organizational Research Methods*, 16(2), 270–301.

Cook, T. D. & Campbell, D. T. (1979). *Quasi-Experimentation: Design and Analysis for Field Settings*. Chicago: Rand McNally.

Doz, Y. L. (1996). The evolution of cooperation in strategic alliances: Initial conditions or learning processes? *Strategic Management Journal*, 17(S1), 55–83.

Eisenhardt, K. M. (1989). Building theories from case study research. *Academy of Management Review*, 14(4), 532–550.

Gibbert, M., Nair, L. B. & Weiss, M. (2014). Oops, I've got an outlier in my data – What now? Using the deviant case method for theory building. In Academy of Management Proceedings, Vol. 2014, No. 1. Briarcliff Manor, NY 10510: Academy of Management, p. 12411.

Gibbert, M., Nair, L. B., Weiss, M. & Hoegl, M. (2021). Using outliers for theory building. *Organizational Research Methods*, 24(1), 172–181.

Giordano, P. C. (1989). *Confronting Control Theory's Negative Cases. Theoretical Integration in the Study of Deviance and Crime: Problems and Prospects*. Albany: State University of New York Press, 261–278.

King, G., Keohane, R. O. & Verba, S. (1994). *Designing Social Inquiry*. Princeton: Princeton University Press.

Kundera, M. (1989). *The Art of the Novel*. New York: Harper Perennial Modern Classics.

Robinson, J. A. & Acemoglu, D. (2012). *Why Nations Fail: The Origins of Power, Prosperity and Poverty*. London: Profile Books.

Sullivan, C. J. (2011). The utility of the deviant case in the development of criminological theory. *Criminology*, 49(3), 905–920.

Yin, R. K. (2003). *Case Study Research: Design and Methods*. Thousand Oaks: Sage.

Zott, C. & Huy, Q. N. (2007). How entrepreneurs use symbolic management to acquire resources. *Administrative Science Quarterly*, 52(1), 70–105.

CHAPTER 9

A Parting Note, on an Optimistic Note

Here we are, at the final chapter of this book on case study designs! Up until now, we showcased the different possible case study designs that you can undertake for your own qualitative research. We first discussed the four archetypical case study designs, by highlighting their individual strengths and weaknesses. We then introduced you to our technique of "sequencing case study designs" that could leverage the strengths of individual case study designs through different combinations which suit one's exact research purposes. As such, the sequencing of case study designs acknowledges the simple fact that designs are malleable. How you sequence different case study designs will rest upon your imaginative curiosity.

In this parting chapter, we now focus on methodological considerations and debates that we have touched upon (but not elaborated upon) in the earlier chapters. We also include some new considerations, which were not discussed in earlier chapters (primarily because they were beyond the scope of this book). Nonetheless, in this final "farewell" chapter, we briefly discuss them to affirm their importance, since the eventual goal of the book is to equip you to choose and design your own sequence of case study designs that suits your research needs best. Therefore, in the following sections, we briefly discuss research paradigms, research questions, quality criteria for case study research, data collection, and data analysis. We will then end on a parting but optimistic note on how to sequence your own case study designs.

9.1 Research Paradigms

At this point, we must address how different research paradigms resonate with the case study designs we discuss in this book. But before we discuss this, it is worth asking: what is a research paradigm? Well, a research paradigm can be seen as a set of basic beliefs that interrogates your assumptions of reality and how you seek to measure this reality (Brand, 2009).

163

We are not going to engage in a full discussion on paradigms as it lies beyond the scope of this book. Nonetheless, we discuss the paradigms in the realm of sequencing case study designs by focusing more specifically on the dominant presence and divide between the positivist and interpretivist paradigms (e.g. see Bluhm et al., 2011; Gephart, 2004). The positivist paradigm functions under the assumption of an objective world, which can be explained using objective concepts and propositions (Bonache & Festing, 2020; Gephart, 2004). The interpretivist paradigm, on the other hand, acknowledges the presence of multiple realities which are socially constructed (Brand, 2009; Gephart, 2004). Often, positivism is discussed in connection with quantitative data collection and analysis methods and interpretivism is deliberated in the context of qualitative research (Gephart, 2004). However, qualitative research methods can also follow a positivist approach. Directed qualitative content analysis of textual data is one such example (Nair, 2018).

So now this leads to the big question – Do the different case study (archetypical and sequenced) designs have different implications for users from positivist and interpretivist paradigms? The simple answer is no. These designs are frameworks, which can work across different paradigms. Moreover, these designs do not restrict the user on the data collection or analysis techniques. Depending on the research questions, the designs are flexible enough to incorporate different paradigmatic positions. The readers of this book can hence use their imaginative curiosity to develop a sequenced or archetypical case study design without concerns about whether it would clash with their paradigmatic positions.

9.2   Research Questions

In Chapter 2, we discussed different types of research questions whose functions range from the exploratory to the explanatory. The exploratory research questions focus on what characterizes a particular phenomenon. The explanatory research questions focus specifically on the effect of a particular causal condition on a certain outcome or generally on the causal factors underlying a particular outcome or the resultant outcomes of a particular causal condition. Depending on the research questions one is interested in investigating, a choice between different case study designs can be made. For instance, single holistic designs are contextually sensitive and have high explanatory power for phenomena which occur in a specific context. If a research question requires an examination of the causal conditions underlying a particular outcome in a specific context, a single

Y-focused holistic design is suitable. Instead, if the interest is on understanding the effect of a particular causal condition in a specific context, a single X-focused holistic design can be used. Likewise, single holistic designs can also explore the characteristics of a research phenomenon at a given context in a given time.

However, if the researcher aims to understand the influence of the causal conditions on outcomes across multiple similar contexts, a multiple holistic design with literal replication might be a better option. This design ensures that the study results are reliable across a range of similar cases. Likewise, to understand the impact of causal conditions across different contexts, a multiple holistic design with theoretical replication will be useful. In these scenarios, it is important to ensure that the replicated contexts are naturally controlled to allow for the comparison. Therefore, case selection should be done purposefully with the intention to select a case(s) that best suits the needs of the research (as discussed in Chapter 5). Multiple holistic designs can also be used for exploratory research questions if the focus of the study is on exploring the constituents of a particular phenomenon in different contexts.

Single embedded designs can be useful in the case of research questions exploring a phenomenon over time and tracing its antecedents or consequences. In particular, a longitudinal single embedded design will have higher internal validity due to its naturalistic control of the research context. Cross-sectional single embedded designs can explore the constituents and the causal conditions/consequences of a particular phenomenon across different sub-cases. Due to their embedded nature, cross-sectional designs have higher external validity than single holistic designs. Multiple embedded designs are more sophisticated than the single embedded designs and the holistic designs since they allow for replication at different levels. Depending on the research question, multiple embedded designs can conduct literal and theoretical replication within the cases (i.e. replication across sub-cases) or between the cases (i.e. replication across cases).

Your research question will play an important role not only in determining which individual case study design suits your research needs best, but also in any potential sequencing of case study designs. In fact, as you iterate between your data and analysis, your imaginative curiosity might get intrigued with newer research questions or sub-questions that you might want to follow up on with another case study design. Hence, the choice of the suitable case study design rests on the research question, which is why we discuss this well-discussed topic (in Chapter 2) here again!

Apart from the research question, the researcher also has to ensure that case studies are conducted in a rigorous manner. We have already seen different criteria of rigor in the former chapters. Here we keep our discussion limited to two of the rigor criteria (internal and external validity). Furthermore, we discuss the interpretivist notion of trustworthiness by introducing two of its criteria (credibility and transferability). We then go on to discuss in more detail what qualitative case study researchers can do to ensure that the rigor/trustworthiness criteria are implemented. Let us warn you – the use of rigor/trustworthiness criteria as quality checks is highly contested in qualitative case study research (Gibbert et al., 2008).

9.3   Quality Criteria for Case Study Research: Rigor and Trustworthiness

There are multiple ways of ensuring the quality of case study research. Rigor and trustworthiness are two notions suggested by prior research for this purpose. In this book, we have so far discussed the rigor criteria. However, rigor is not the only framework used for ascertaining the quality of a case study. Hence, here we discuss both the rigor and its interpretivist counterpart, namely trustworthiness. Rigor is based on the "natural science model" (e.g. Eisenhardt & Graebner, 2007; Piekkari et al., 2009). This model involves four criteria: Construct validity, internal validity, external validity, and reliability (Behling, 1980; Campbell & Stanley, 1963; Cook & Campbell, 1979a, 1979b). The positivist stream of qualitative researchers has welcomed this classification of rigor openheartedly. The positive link between scholarly impact and rigorous research has been explored in various disciplines, including management (Gibbert & Ruigrok, 2010; Gibbert et al., 2008). Yin (2013), as well as some other scholars from different paradigmatic traditions (e.g., Campbell, 1975; Denzin & Lincoln, 1994; Eisenhardt, 1989; Kidder & Judd, 1986; Kirk & Miller, 1986; Silverman, 2005, 2006; Stake, 1995) have adopted this positivist model of case study quality. This suggests that, although rigor is a positivist notion, the underlying research actions which contribute to a rigorous study are also applied in many interpretivist studies.

However, many nonpositivist qualitative researchers do not agree with this classification. As a substitute to the natural science model, these researchers suggest an interpretivist framework of trustworthiness which entails credibility, transferability, dependability, and confirmability. Credibility, similar to internal validity, discusses the confidence of the research findings. It examines whether the research findings are based on correct interpretations of the participants' actual experiences and views. In other words, it examines the congruence of a study's findings with the reality (Merriam, 1998). Transferability examines the extent to which the results of a study can be transferred to other contexts or populations. This is similar to the positivist notion of external validity/generalizability. What is surprising is that, even in the case of the interpretivist trustworthiness, transferability is prioritized in research reports over credibility (Nair, 2021; Nair and Gibbert, 2016). We focus more deeply on the criteria of internal and external validity (or their interpretivist counterparts of credibility and transferability) since these are the ones which are most contested and discussed in the context of qualitative case study research.

9.3.1 The Internal versus External Validity Debate

Case study research has often been criticized for its lack of external validity. Unlike large-N studies using random sampling, small-N studies involving case study research are not representative of the larger, unexplored population. For instance, the classic case study of Middletown that we discussed in Chapter 2 might not be representative of all typical US cities. Hence, the lack of external validity is indeed a weakness of case study research. However, this focus on external validity in the context of case study research is an underappreciation of the strength of case study research (i.e. its internal validity). The strength of a purported relationship between a causal condition and outcome pertains to the study's internal validity rather than its external validity, thus making the former the more fundamental form of rigor (Cook & Campbell, 1979b; Gibbert & Ruigrok, 2010). Due to methodological literature focusing more predominantly on external validity rather than internal validity, the latter is often neglected at the expense of the former (Gibbert et al., 2008). External validity is treated as a godsend which represents methodological rigor in its totality, although that is far from the truth in the context of case study research. For instance, in the management discipline, Gibbert and Ruigrok (2010) identified that external validity was the more predominantly reported rigor criteria in case study research in comparison to internal validity, in the top journals over a period of six years.

In this book, we suggest that case study researchers focus on the strength of case study research, that is its internal validity, more predominantly before aiming for external validity. If one cannot account for the causality of a relationship within the context of his/her own study, any attempts to generalize it beyond the study would be futile. Particularly since case studies are more commonly used in early stages of theory development, an internal validity problem would have ripple effects on the rigor and overall quality of the whole sequence of case study designs. Resultantly, this will detriment the quality of the involved findings and any subsequent studies depending or building on it. Internal validity is thus the strength of a high-quality case study design, followed by its analytical generalization potential (i.e. its potential to generalize to previously developed theories). We suggest some solid research actions for ensuring internal and external validity in the following sections (in the respective order of importance).

9.3.1.1   Internal Validity

This criterion refers to the causal relationships between variables and results (e.g. by Cook & Campbell, 1979b; Yin, 2013). For ensuring the internal validity of a study, the case study researcher must provide a plausible causal argument, along with a compelling and strong logical reasoning that can defend the research conclusions. Internal validity mostly pertains to the data analysis phase of case studies (Yin, 2013). Specifically, three research actions can be performed to enhance the internal validity of a case study design. First, we need to formulate a clear research framework which is capable of demonstrating that the independent variable (i.e. causal condition) X leads to the dependent variables (i.e. outcome) Y. The framework should also ensure that the dependent variable(s) are not due to the presence of any conditions unaccounted for. Secondly, by combining inputs from different theories through theory triangulation, the researcher can observe and verify the findings of a particular case study from multiple perspectives (Yin, 2013). Lastly, the researchers can match the patterns observed in the case study with predicted patterns from prior literature or from previous studies in different contexts to ensure that their findings possess internal validity (Denzin & Lincoln, 1994; Eisenhardt, 1989). Once the study's internal validity is ensured, the researcher can move on to check whether his/her study is externally valid. The focus here should not be on statistical generalization (i.e. generalization to the population) but on analytic generalization (i.e. generalization to prior theories).

9.3.1.2   External Validity

Otherwise known as "generalizability," "external validity" is the other quality criteria that we are interested in discussing. For a theory to be externally valid, it must be applicable not only in the research setting in which the study was conducted, but also in other settings which deal with the same phenomenon (e.g. Calder et al., 1982). It is important to manage expectations at this point and admit that case study research does not aim to achieve statistical generalization. The main aim of case studies is not to be representative of or infer conclusions about an entire population (Gerring, 2008; Yin, 2013). However, case studies entail another type of generalization (i.e. the analytical generalization), which refers to generalization from empirical observations to theory, rather than to a population (e.g. Yin, 2013). Since the aim is to generalize to a theory (Yin, 2013), individual case study designs can add to the analytical generalizability. Analytical generalization can also be achieved through cross-case comparison (Eisenhardt, 1989) and by sequencing case study designs. Apart from comparisons, the researchers should also ensure that they transparently provide a clear rationale for the case study selection and sufficient details of the case study context in the final report, so that the reader can appreciate the researchers' methodological choices and hence be convinced of the generalizability potential of the study (Cook & Campbell 1979b).

9.4   Iterative Cycle of Data Collection and Data Analysis

A final note is due on data collection and data analysis, which are integral parts of any qualitative case study. When it comes to qualitative research, there are multiple ways in which you can undertake data collection and analysis. However, an important aspect of qualitative research that also sets it apart from its quantitative counterparts is the capacity to undertake data collection and data analysis simultaneously. This back and forth movement allows researchers to readjust their research process when new insights might prompt a sequencing or readjustment of an existing case study design (as indicated in Chapter 7).

When it comes to data collection, depending on his/her needs, a researcher can rely on a variety of data sources. In fact, qualitative researchers take pride in the number of hours spent writing field notes and making observations in the field. Moreover, qualitative researchers also rely on interviews and focus group discussions, during which they ask questions or facilitate discussions with research participants. The participants are individuals experiencing or observing the phenomenon of interest who gave their consent to be part of the study and subsequently are willing to discuss their perspectives on the phenomenon. There are also several other data sources that a qualitative researcher can use. Secondary data sources such as archival documents, videos, autobiographies, tweets, etc., are some of them. For enhancing the rigor of a case study, a researcher can apply data triangulation, i.e. he/she can triangulate different data sources to corroborate the involved study's findings.

BUT BEFORE WE MOVE ON LET'S WATCH …

… ANNA ROSLING RÖNNLUND'S TED TALK: "SEE HOW THE REST OF THE WORLD LIVES, ORGANIZED BY INCOME"
Answer the following questions:

Q.1   What data is Anna analyzing? How is this data different from data collected through interviews and focus group discussions? What are the advantages and disadvantages of using this type of data?
Q.2   Will you incorporate this type of data in your data collection? Explain.

BUT BEFORE WE MOVE ON LET'S ALSO WATCH …

… ERNESTO SIROLLI'S TED TALK: "WANT TO HELP SOMEONE? SHUT UP AND LISTEN!"
After watching the TED talk, please answer the following questions:

Q.1   How was the system of "Enterprise facilitation" different?
Q.2   Why do you think it is important to "shut up and listen!"?
Q.3   How will you incorporate learnings from Ernesto Sirolli's TED talk in your data collection?

Regarding data analysis, a qualitative case study researcher can apply different analysis techniques. To name a few there is qualitative content analysis (Hsieh & Shannon, 2005; Nair, 2018), thematic analysis (Attride-Stirling, 2001), and rhetorical analysis (Gross, 1990). The general idea behind qualitative analysis techniques is categorizing and reordering the massive data into meaningful theoretical categories. These analysis techniques can hence be viewed as data reduction procedures (e.g. see the discussion on data structure by Gioia et al. (2013)). Depending upon the specific objectives of the study, data analysis techniques with different specific purposes can be used.

9.5   Sequencing Case Study Designs for Your Own Research

The ultimate aim of this book is to empower you with the necessary understanding of the different ways in which case study research can be designed. We would like you to use your imaginative curiosity and formulate your very own sequence of case study designs which will help you to achieve your specific research objectives,

It is our strong conviction that this sequencing of case study designs can only materialize once there is a sound understanding of the specific strengths and weaknesses of the individual case study designs. It is only through a thorough consideration of the strengths and weaknesses of individual designs that you can arrive at an optimal combination of them. Hence, here we provide a brief summary of the strengths and weaknesses of individual case study designs, along with the different decisions that are important for sequencing case study designs. See Figure 9.1 for this guiding framework.

It is important here that we caution you on the possible misuse of the proposed guiding framework for sequencing case study designs. What does "misuse" mean in this context? Well, it simply means that, while you take guidance and inspiration from this framework, you should not limit your imaginative curiosity to the confinements of this guiding framework. In fact, you can adopt and adapt it based on the challenges and requirements of your research study (Nair, 2021). We believe that coupling our guiding framework on sequencing case study designs with your own imaginative curiosity will help in identifying diverse ways of designing qualitative case study research. After all, qualitative research is all about this pluralism.

BUT BEFORE WE MOVE ON LET'S THINK ABOUT ...

... PLURALISTIC CASE STUDY DESIGNS

For this short exercise, we want you to think about the following question:

Q.   What are the benefits and disadvantages of pluralistic case study designs?

We strongly root for pluralistic case study designs (and in general for pluralistic research) primarily because it allows a researcher to take on a multi-faceted approach towards understanding the phenomenon of interest. As we discussed in our earlier chapters (more specifically in Chapters 7 and 8), when we engage in a plurality of designs, it helps us to see a fuller

Case study design #1

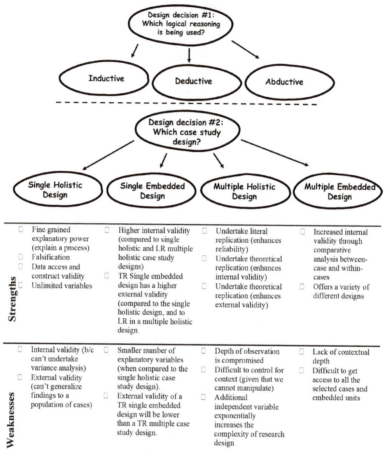

	Single Holistic Design	Single Embedded Design	Multiple Holistic Design	Multiple Embedded Design
Strengths	□ Fine grained explanatory power (explain a process) □ Falsification □ Data access and construct validity □ Unlimited variables	□ Higher internal validity (compared to single holistic and LR multiple holistic case study designs) □ TR Single embedded design has a higher external validity (compared to the single holistic design, and to LR in a multiple holistic design.	□ Undertake literal replication (enhances reliability) □ Undertake theoretical replication (enhances internal validity) □ Undertake theoretical replication (enhances external validity)	□ Increased internal validity through comparative analysis between-case and within-cases □ Offers a variety of different designs
Weaknesses	□ Internal validity (b/c can't undertake variance analysis) □ External validity (can't generalize findings to a population of cases)	□ Smaller number of explanatory variables (when compared to the single holistic case study design). □ External validity of a TR single embedded design will be lower than a TR multiple case study design.	□ Depth of observation is compromised □ Difficult to control for context (given that we cannot manipulate) □ Additional independent variable exponentially increases the complexity of research design	□ Lack of contextual depth □ Difficult to get access to all the selected cases and embedded units

You can continue applying the considerations above for the next case study design

Figure 9.1   A guiding framework for sequencing case study designs

and more complete picture of the phenomenon, by allowing for a more comprehensive sensemaking process (Delbridge & Fiss, 2013). In fact, we wouldn't shy away from making a "sweeping" claim that it is through this openness and acceptance of pluralistic case study designs (and even research) that we can expect to solve some of the most pressing global problems (e.g. climate change, poverty, inequality). We see, therefore, much value in being inclusive of different designs and encourage you to adapt and take inspiration from our guiding framework to sequence your case study designs in a way that suits your research needs the best possible way.

REFERENCES

Attride-Stirling, J. (2001). Thematic networks: An analytic tool for qualitative research. *Qualitative Research*, 1(3), 385–405.

Behling, O. (1980). The case for the natural science model for research in organizational behavior and organization theory. *Academy of Management Review*, 5(4), 483–490.

Bluhm, D. J., Harman, W., Lee, T. W. & Mitchell, T. R. (2011). Qualitative research in management: A decade of progress. *Journal of Management Studies*, 48(8), 1866–1891.

Bonache, J. & Festing, M. (2020). Research paradigms in international human resource management: An epistemological systematisation of the field. *German Journal of Human Resource Management*, 34(2), 99–123.

Brand, V. (2009). Empirical business ethics research and paradigm analysis. *Journal of Business Ethics*, 86(4), 429–449.

Calder, B. J., Phillips, L. W. & Tybout, A. M. (1982). The concept of external validity. *Journal of Consumer Research*, 9(3), 240–244.

Campbell, D. T. (1975). Degrees of freedom and the case study. *Comparative Political Studies*, 8(2): 178–193.

Campbell, D. T. & Stanley, J. (1963). *Experimental and Quasi Experimental Designs for Research*. Boston: Houghton Mifflin.

Cook, T. D. & Campbell, D. T. (1979a). The design and conduct of true experiments and quasi-experiments in field settings. In *Reproduced in part in Research in Organizations: Issues and Controversies*. Santa Monica: Goodyear Publishing Company.

(1979b). *Quasi-Experimentation: Design and Analysis Issues for Field Settings*. Chicago: Rand McNally.

Delbridge, R. & Fiss, P. C. (eds.) (2013). Editors' comments: Styles of theorizing and the social organization of knowledge. *Academy of Management Review*, 38(3), 325–331.

Denzin, N. K. & Lincoln, Y. S. (1994). *Handbook of Qualitative Research*. Thousand Oaks: Sage.

Eisenhardt, K. M. (1989). Building theories from case study research. *Academy of Management Review*, 14(4), 532–550.

Eisenhardt, K. M. & Graebner, M. E. (2007). Theory building from cases: Opportunities and challenges. *Academy of Management Journal*, 50(1), 25–32.

Gephart Jr, R. P. (2004). Qualitative research and the Academy of Management Journal. *Academy of Management Journal*, 47(4), 454–462.

Gerring, J. (2008). Case selection for case-study analysis: Qualitative and quantitative techniques. In J. M. Box-Steffensmeier, H. E. Brady & D. Collier (eds.) *The Oxford Handbook of Political Methodology*. New York: Oxford University Press, 647–648.

Gibbert, M. & Ruigrok, W. (2010). The "what" and "how" of case study rigor: Three strategies based on published work. *Organizational Research Methods*, 13(4), 710–737.

Gibbert, M., Ruigrok, W. & Wicki, B. (2008). What passes as a rigorous case study? *Strategic Management Journal*, 29(13), 1465–1474.

Gioia, D. A., Corley, K. G. & Hamilton, A. L. (2013). Seeking qualitative rigor in inductive research: Notes on the Gioia methodology. *Organizational Research Methods*, 16(1), 15–31.

Gross, A. G. (1990). *The Rhetoric of Science*. Cambridge, MA: Harvard University Press.

Hsieh, H. F. & Shannon, S. E. (2005). Three approaches to qualitative content analysis. *Qualitative Health Research*, 15(9), 1277–1288.

Kidder, L. & Judd, C. M. (1986). *Research Methods in Social Relations*, 5th ed. New York: Holt, Rinehart & Winston.

Kirk, J. & Miller, M. L. (1986). *Reliability and Validity in Qualitative Research*. London: Sage.

Merriam, S. B. (1998). *Qualitative Research and Case Study Applications in Education. Revised and expanded from "Case Study Research in Education."* San Francisco: Jossey-Bass Publishers.

Nair, L. B. (2018). *Appraising Scholarly Impact Using Directed Qualitative Content Analysis: A Study of Article Title Attributes in Management Research*. Thousand Oaks: Sage.

(2021). To discard or to ado(a)pt? Looking at qualitative research templates through the lens of organizational routines. *Qualitative Research in Organizations and Management*, 16(2), 409–423.

Nair, L. B. & Gibbert, M. (2016). Hot on the audit trail: How to assess methodological transparency of grounded theory in management? Academy of Management Annual Meeting. Anaheim, USA, August 2016.

Piekkari, R., Welch, C. & Paavileinen, E. (2009). The case study as disciplinary convention: Evidence from international business journals. *Organizational Research Methods*, 12(3), 567–589.

Silverman, D. (2005). *Doing Qualitative Research*. London: Sage.

(2006). *Interpreting Qualitative Data*. London: Sage.

Stake, R. E. (1995). *The Art of Case Study Research*. Thousand Oaks: Sage.

Yin, R. K. (2013). *Case Study Research: Design and Methods*. Thousand Oaks: Sage.

Index

Index

replication. *See also* literal replication; theoretical
    replication
  in multiple holistic designs, 81–82
  in single embedded designs, 81–82
  in theoretical sampling technique, 83–84
replication crisis, 54–55
replication logic, 50
research questions, 11–23, 164–166
  abduction and, 25–28
  classification of, 11
  deduction and, 25–28
  descriptive, 11
  emancipatory, 11
  evaluative, 11
  explanatory, 19–23
    context for, 24–25
    X and Y-centered, 21–23
    X-centered, 21
    Y-centered, 20
    Z variable in, 23–24
  exploratory, 13–18
    X-focused, 13
    Y-focused, 13
  formulation of, 11
  generative, 11
  induction and, 25–28
  in inductive-deductive sequencing, 133–135
  Mill's method of difference, 24
  in multiple embedded designs, 165
  objectives of, 13–17
  observational-relational, 11
  qualitative, 11
  quantitative, 11
  in single embedded designs, 165
  variables in, 12–13
  in Zott and Huy case study, 153–155
"A Review" (Ericksen), 52–53
rigor, of case study research, 166–167
Robinson, J. A., 61, 147
Rönnlund, Anna Rosling, 170

sampling
  for single embedded designs, 82–84
    purposeful sampling, 84
    theoretical sampling, 83–84
sampling bias
  literal replication and, 59–60
  in single holistic designs, 44
selection bias, in single holistic designs, 43
sequencing, in case study design, 5, 171–173. *See
    also* deductive-inductive sequencing;
    inductive-deductive sequencing
  abductive approach to, 126–127
  benefits of, 124–125
  conceptual approach to, 122–124

  definition of, 124–131
  framework for, 172
  as iterative process, 129–130
  reporting of, 140–142
  scope of, 124–131
  theoretical saturation in, 127
  visual representation of, 128
single embedded designs, 5, 32, 95
  cross-sectional, 85–89, 94–96
    psychological applications for, 87–88
    thinking exercises for, 88
  definition of, 78–80
  longitudinal, 85, 89–96
    jigsaw processes in, 92–93
    theoretical replication in, 90
  multiple holistic design compared to, 80–82
    level of analysis, 80–81
    nature of replication, 81–82
    within-case comparison, 82
  purpose of, 78–80
  replication in
    multiple holistic design compared to, 81–82
    in theoretical sampling technique, 83–84
  research questions in, 165
  sampling for, 82–84
    purposeful, 84
    theoretical, 83–84
  selection rationale for, 82–84
    phenomenon-driven, 83
    selection techniques, 83
    theoretical sampling for, 83–84
    theory-driven, 83
  single holistic design compared to, 80–82
    level of analysis, 80–81
    nature of replication, 81–82
    within-case comparison, 82
  strengths of, 96–100
    external validity, 97
    internal validity, 96–97
  weaknesses of, 97–100
    external validity, 99
    lack of explanatory variables, 97–99
single holistic designs, 5
  black-swan moments in, 45
  causal process tracing in, 33
  causes in, 37–39
  conceptual approach to, 31–33
  definition of, 32
  in field management, 34
  governmental politics model, 42
  jigsaw processes in, 35–36
  multiple embedded designs compared to,
    104–105
  naturalistic generalization in, 45
  organizational process model, 42